Her routine on the asymmetric bars, performed with just the right amount of control and flair, drew a gasp from the crowd for its daring. Even the rival gymnasts were clapping when she landed. Everyone watched the scoreboard beside the bars. A wait, and then the figures which were to make Olympic history . . .

This is the story of how a fourteen-year-old Rumanian girl confounded the Olympic results computer and was dubbed Little Miss Perfect by the world's press. It tells how she got there – the gruelling daily training, the contests which started when she was only seven, the lost childhood and the disappointments – and it tells where she went afterwards . . .

D1719364

## THE AUTHOR

Cliff Temple covers major athletics and gymnastics events for *The Sunday Times*. Cliff attended the 1972 Munich and 1976 Montreal Olympic Games in this capacity, and contributes to a number of gymnastics magazines. He is also the co-author of a very successful coaching book for young gymnasts.

His own sporting activity centres on long-distance running, and he lives with his wife at Sandgate, near Folkestone.

# Nadia Comaneci

## The Enchanting Story of
## Little Miss Perfect

### CLIFF TEMPLE

**EVEREST BOOKS LTD**
4 Valentine Place, London SE1

Published in Great Britain by Everest Books Ltd, 1977
A paperback original
ISBN 0905018 788

## Chapter One

## 'WHO IS THIS NADIA WHATSIT?'

Perfection is something to which millions of sportsmen and women aspire, but which only a handful of individuals among them actually achieve. Usually it takes a very long time. Yet Nadia Comaneci was just fourteen years and eight months when she demonstrated gymnastic perfection to the world on an occasion when many more experienced competitors in all sports have come to unexpected grief: the Olympic Games.

Before July 1976 her name was known only to a few people outside gymnastics. She had been seen just once in Britain, and her second scheduled appearance, at the inaugural World Cup contest at Wembley in October 1975, was cancelled when she suffered an injury in her native Rumania.

Although Nadia's victory in the 1975 European championships in Norway, at the age of just thirteen, had set the gymnastics world alight, it was only scantily reported in Britain and elsewhere. The big name, the one everyone knew, was still that of Olga Korbut, the tiny Russian who had captured the hearts of millions of television viewers during the 1972 Munich Olympics, and at displays and championships ever since.

So as the world's attention began to turn towards Montreal, and the XXI Olympic Games, in the summer of 1976, the questions most armchair spectators were asking were: 'How will Olga Korbut get on this time?' and: 'How will the reigning Olympic champion Ludmila Tourischeva fare?' Only a few asked: 'Who is this Nadia Whatsit some of the sports journalists keep on about?'

At home in Rumania, Nadia and her young teammates were packing their cases, ready to set out for the biggest competition of their lives. They were still young, but the road up to this point had already been a hard one. Nadia's coaches, Marta and Bela Karolyi, had been putting the finishing touches to the routines which they hoped would, in Montreal, challenge Russian domination and put Rumanian gymnastics well and truly on the map.

Around the world, gymnastics judges with many years experience were also packing their bags for the Olympics. More than most people, they knew that the battle for Olympic medals between the Soviet girls and the Rumanians was going to be a fierce one. But they could not know that little Nadia Comaneci was going to put on a show which would cause them to award her an unprecedented total of seven 'perfect' scores of ten out of ten, and that Nadia was going to spark off a whole new controversy over a possible revised scoring system.

The present scoring system just did not allow for perfection. Even the electronic scoreboards which would be set up in the Olympic arena would not have the space to display '10·00' – only '9·95' at the most. After all, whoever scored ten in the Olympics?

The answer was Nadia Comaneci. Not once, but seven times. Such would be the tremendously high standard and rivalry that one of the Russian gymnasts, Nelli Kim, would also score ten twice. But although Kim, Tourischeva and Korbut were stars on the Olympic podium, Nadia would be the superstar.

She was the gymnast who would silence the 16,000 crowd just by stepping up to a piece of apparatus, and throughout whose performance everyone would maintain a kind of reverent hush, so that even if another gymnast finished on a different piece of apparatus, which normally evokes applause, the arena would remain silent. All eyes would be on Nadia.

At the end of the Olympic gymnastics tournament, Nadia would have gold medals for the asymmetric bars, the beam, and the individual combined exercises. She would have a silver medal from the team competition, and a bronze from the floor exercise.

But above all she would have shown a standard of coolness, agility and courage which would have been admirable in a gymnast of far greater experience and maturity, let alone a fourteen-year-old schoolgirl. No longer would the world have to ask 'Who is this Nadia Whatsit?' She was Little Miss Perfect.

*Chapter Two*

## 'AH, BUT NADIA NEVER FALLS'

The road to Olympic success is never a short one, and it often involves climbing a great many hills. For, despite her youth, Nadia had been training – and training hard – for more than seven years before her Montreal triumphs. Indeed, the whole of her day-to-day life has been built around gymnastics.

Whether she will eventually feel that much of her childhood has been lost in the gymnasium, which is an assumption many people have been ready to make for her, is something which only Nadia herself will be able to answer – but not this year, or next year, or perhaps before 1990 when she may be able to look back and put everything into perspective.

But if she has lost her childhood years, she has instead achieved something which only one in many millions of sportsmen and women ever manage: totally to dominate their sport, to the extent of adding a dimension to what was previously thought possible. The athlete or swimmer has far more scope to change normal standards by exceeding records measured in seconds and inches, but the gymnast is more limited by what the mind can visualize and the body can execute.

Yet Nadia managed to bring fresh elements not only of courage and daring, but also perfection, to a sport which will consequently never be the same again. There were moments in Montreal, I must admit, when some of us covering gymnastics were waiting with pens poised for the moment when a chink would show through the armour, and Nadia would bungle something, ending up in an undignified heap on the floor.

'Come on, kid,' shouted one veteran American journalist sitting near me on the final day. 'Show us you're human, and fall on your ass just once!' But she didn't.

Instead, she was word perfect. Her routines on the asymmetric bars always looked like an action replay of her faultless display the day before, because they were so consistent and controlled.

Even those people at home who spent most of the Olympic period grumbling that their favourite TV programme had been moved to make way for yet more action from Montreal must have been impressed with her ability, and wondered who she was, where she came from, and how she managed such incredible aerial feats in the gymnastics events – 'swimming in an ocean of air', as one American television commentator described it.

So who *is* Nadia Elena Comaneci (pronounced Comman-etch), gymnast supreme, and how did she become, at fourteen years old, a worldwide sporting celebrity?

To the gymnastics world she is a phenomenon, who condensed whole years of experience and ability into month-long packages, until she had caught up with the best internationals even before she was in her teens. Then she kept on going.

To her parents, in the town of Gheorghe Gheorghiu-

Dej, Rumania, she is a daughter born with so much energy to spare that as a four-year-old she was already jumping around on the furniture like a frustrated trampolinist, a small bundle of restlessness.

In fact, they were delighted when she finally began gymnastics at school at the age of six, but if it had not been for her natural reservoir of tireless movement, Nadia might never have been able to cope with the amount of training which she later undertook.

Now, for instance, a typical day begins at 7 a.m., when she gets up, has breakfast, and then walks the half-mile to school. The Comaneci family – her mother, who works in an office, her father, who is a car mechanic, and her brother Adrian, four years younger than Nadia – live in a state worker's flat near the centre of Gheorghe Gheorghiu-Dej.

The town, with a population of more than 40,000, nestles in the foothills of the Carpathian Mountains, near Bacau, and was originally called Onesti, until being re-named after a Communist party leader some years ago.

Nadia was born there, and she calls it 'the most beautiful town in the world'. With its boulevards and architectural complexes, it was chiefly known until recently as a petrochemistry citadel, but lately it has achieved fame as being 'Nadia Comaneci's home town'.

At school, the morning is spent on academic subjects, with chemistry, French and English being among Nadia's favourites, although sometimes she looks as puzzled as any pupil anywhere in the world, as she chews the end of her pen and tries to think of the

English for 'door'. In the English lessons, not a word of Rumanian is spoken.

Then after her morning lessons, she goes home for lunch and sleeps for two hours or so in the afternoon to allow her body the extra rest it needs to cope with the hard physical demands of gymnastics training.

After that it is a return to school, only this time the subject is gymnastics, and the classroom is the gymnasium. Three or four hours a day are spent in training with coaches Marta and Bela Karolyi, along with other members of the national team, who are now based here under the Karolyis' guidance. These training sessions take place six days a week, with a rest only on Sundays.

Then Nadia goes home for a late supper around 8 p.m., before getting down to her homework – academic subjects and gymnastics theory, both of which are given equal importance at this rather unusual school. And then next day, at 7 a.m., the routine begins all over again.

There are holidays, of course, but the gymnastics training rarely stops. Nadia's best friend is Teodora Ungureanu, a locksmith's daughter from the same town, who is a year older than Nadia, but shares her love of gymnastics and lives to the same timetable. At Montreal, Teodora was also a gymnastics medallist. They, and their other gymnast schoolmates, have spent years perfecting exercises in the gym, but when they have some free time, they enjoy cycling, swimming, and climbing the various playground apparatus in the local pleasure park.

There, from the top of the Devil's Wheel (a smaller version of the fairground Big Wheel) they can see the whole town. On other days, they go to the seaside, or on visits to the nearby Uzu Valley. In winter, when snow covers Gheorghe Gheorghiu-Dej, they go tobogganing and skiing. Their lives are constantly active ones.

There have been rumours, unsubstantiated, that sometimes gymnasts are given special pills to delay the onset of puberty, so that they will retain their boy-like bodies, all flat chests and rib-cages, for as long as possible. But if this does not apply to the Rumanians, certainly they seem caught between a slow-motion of their childhood (Nadia sleeps with her favourite doll, and in Montreal carried a stuffed toy everywhere with her) and a speeded-up version of their potential gymnastic life. Something has to go.

Boyfriends, in the romantic sense, had not entered Nadia's life by the time of the Montreal Olympics, although the year before she had even received a proposal of marriage at the age of thirteen from a boy fan, who wrote: 'I am asking for your hand when I am grown up. You must know I have asked Father's permission and he agrees.'

Nadia's own favourite male is Alain Delon, the French actor, but dolls rather than the cinema are her hobby. She has collected more than two hundred of them, many in national costume and gathered while on trips abroad.

She does not yet, outwardly (nor apparently inwardly) have anything like the range of emotions of an Olga Korbut. At Montreal she was small (just under five feet tall, and weighing 6 stones 2 pounds), with a serious face but one which was young even for her tender years. She has brown eyes, wears her long brown hair either in bunches or a pony tail, and there is a small mole on her left cheek. Most of the time in Montreal she was expressionless. Sometimes she smiled, but we hardly ever saw her laugh.

'I know how to laugh and to smile,' she explained, 'but I do these things after my mission has been completed.'

In Montreal, laughter seemed to be something she shared only with Teodora and their other friends, when there was an air of conspiracy or communal amusement at all these grown-up people rushing around with television cameras, microphones and cameras, trying to catch her every word. It was as if everyone else was in some sort of dream world, exaggerating what to them was normality, with only their little group really seeing how ridiculous it all was.

At one of the Press conferences in Montreal, someone pursuing the line of 'poor little deprived girl' asked when she had last been able to eat some chocolate. Presumably he wanted her to say: 'Chocolate? What's that? Under our state system I am only allowed bread and water.' In fact, she answered that she had eaten a bar of chocolate that very morning, and you didn't need to be a mind reader to see that she was thinking: 'What a daft question!'

However, she is not allowed to eat too much chocolate. The gymnasts are kept on a diet, with a basis of fruit, milk, cheese and protein. Nadia drinks about four pints of milk a day.

At home in Gheorghe Gheorghiu-Dej, she is naturally a local heroine, and admits that she even has

13

to refuse offers to jump to the head of the queue when she is in the grocer's or the baker's. But everything that she has achieved, for herself, her family, her town, and her country, revolves around the work done in training with the Karolyis. The talent is Nadia's, but without the constant efforts of the coaches, it would have been wasted.

Bela Karolyi is a big man who, next to Nadia, looks like a giant. Although he and his wife share responsibility, it is he who has dreamed up most of Nadia's most difficult technical moves, the ones which catch the imagination, like the 'Salto Comaneci', named after her. In this daring move, she lets go of the high bar in a forward motion, does a half twist and turns it into a back somersault to dismount. No other girl in the world can do it, says Karolyi. Another Olympic gymnast called it 'madness'.

Karolyi says that Nadia has many great assets. Physically, she has strength, speed and flexibility. Mentally, she has intelligence, phenomenal powers of concentration and courage. But the technical purity of her performance is her most brilliant characteristic.

'She likes to work. She is always the first to warm up and she does everything I tell her. She is the best gymnast in the world, and she will improve with the addition of new and different elements.

'Every year we try to put in new exercises. Some are technically too difficult, so we put them away and try again later. We want to develop perfection, towards the time when she gets ten out of ten in every part of the same competition.'

Nadia agrees: 'This is my final goal,' she says. 'To

get the perfect score in every event.'

'This concentration she has,' says Karolyi, 'explains why she never seems to smile. What the public are seeing is concentration so intense that there is no room for anything else. When I am teaching her a new trick, perhaps one which no one else has ever tried, she learns it quickly, just by these powers of concentration.'

One of the sights people first got used to with the appearance of Nadia in international gymnastics, was of this tiny slip of a girl listening gravely to what the towering figure of Karolyi was telling her as they stood beside the podium. Every so often she would nod, and then go off to perform on the apparatus, remembering everything he had told her. The crowd, in Nadia's mind, did not exist at that moment. All that mattered was getting the exercise right, and the more dangerous the moves, the more that concentration was needed.

This is expecially true on the asymmetric bars, where there is the greatest risk in some of Nadia's routines. On the floor exercise, the vault or the beam, she could still hurt herself, but if anything were to go wrong on the bars, with her breathtaking jumps and somersaults between the high and low bar, she could injure herself very severely.

Yet it is typical of her courage that she names the bars as her favourite piece of apparatus 'because of their challenge'. It was also on the bars that she most consistently demonstrated perfection.

Just what is it that gives her this courage? In the U.S. magazine *International Gymnast*, psychologist Dr Joe Massimo put forward a theory based on an interview with Karolyi and Nadia in which he suggested that they have between them transcended belief in the possibility that anything could go wrong.

For instance, when Nadia was asked if she was ever afraid, she replied 'Never!' and really meant it.

Later Karolyi was asked if he was aware how much danger Nadia was really in, performing such daring antics on the bars. 'Ah, but Nadia never falls,' he said, as if that was the end of any further conversation, because the possibility of falling – whatever it meant to anyone else – just did not apply to them. They were above that. Kidology? Perhaps. But it certainly seemed to have worked.

Also, of course, it had been built up over seven years, from the time Nadia first started 'playing' with the apparatus in the gym to get used to it. In fact, it had been built up from a time, in the late 1960s, when a chain of events had first brought the Karolyis and Nadia together.

*Chapter Three*

## DISCOVERY OF A STAR

Nadia, who was born on 12 November 1961, was only seven years old when the gymnastics career, which was to lead to the top step of the Olympic rostrum eight years later, began. She was attending the local primary school in Gheorghe Gheorghiu-Dej, and in the playground at break she and a friend used to pretend to be gymnasts.

It was a time when Rumania's international gymnastics itself had been going through a very lean spell. Apart from bronze team medals in the 1956 and 1960 Olympics, and a bronze medal for the floor exercise won by Elena Leusteanu in 1956, there had been very little success for the national women's team in the Olympic Games. The government felt something had to be done to improve the situation, and so in 1968 a national gymnastics plan was evolved.

Bearing in mind that any gymnast should start very young, the scheme was that small children with an apparent talent should be trained in special schools, with the aim of reaching their gymnastic peak in the early teens. The 1976 Olympics, whose venue then had not even been decided, was to be the first target for success: a target which at that stage must have looked very far off indeed.

A number of coaches were appointed to look after the

training of the youngsters. And one of them was Bela Karolyi, a former soccer player, who was then twenty seven years old. Karolyi, a qualified P.E. teacher, had only become involved in gymnastics through meeting his wife, Marta.

'She was a gymnast,' he says, 'and since I fell in love with her, I fell in love with her sport.'

Eventually, Karolyi learned more and more about gymnastics until he had shown himself to be highly knowledgeable on the technical aspects, and with his wife gifted in the artistic side of gymnastics, they formed an ambitious and competent coaching partnership.

Karolyi went to the sports school established at Gheorghe Gheorghiu-Dej, and the authorities began their nationwide search for gymnastic talent. Every primary school in the country was ordered to watch out for youngsters who showed outstanding ability or promise in P.E. lessons, and gradually a class was built up. But the girl who was to become the first to break through the Rumanian lack of success, Nadia, was living just a few streets away from the school.

'I used to walk round the town, visiting the playgrounds, looking for youngsters with particular aggression and courage,' says Karolyi. 'That was how I discovered Nadia. I noticed her with a friend, running and jumping, pretending to be gymnasts in the school playtime.

'Then the bell rang and they ran into the building and I lost them. I went into all the classes looking for them, but I didn't see them. I went again next day, and I still couldn't find them. And then I tried a third time. I went into one particular classroom and said "Who likes gymnastics?" and the two girls sprang up and said "We do." One of them began training with us, and is now a very promising ballerina. The other was Nadia. It was an important moment in my life.'

And in Nadia's, of course. She was only seven, but her aggression towards physical activity was showing through. 'She loved to fight. She would fight anyone,' recalls Karolyi. 'She had lots of courage, and she was just the right size – well proportioned, lithe, with no fat on her. I knew that with my guidance she could become a great gymnast.'

As part of their talent-finding, though, the Karolyis give all potential gymnasts a test, consisting of a twenty yards sprint, a long jump, and a walk on the balance beam. 'If they are afraid on the beam, we send them home right away. We only keep those who like it and show good balance.' Nadia was kept.

In less than a year, Nadia had taken part in her first gymnastics competition – the Rumanian National Junior Children's championships, in which she was, still seven, the youngest competitor. She finished thirteenth. 'Because thirteen is an unlucky number,' says Karolyi, 'I bought her an Eskimo doll for good luck, and told her she must never finish thirteenth again.' The following year, Nadia won the title, and that doll, in its faded sealskin dress, now travels to every competition with her. It has certainly brought her luck.

Her work at school, which combined gymnastics training with the ordinary academic subjects, called for more and more time in the gymnasium. She started training for gymnastics just one hour a day, then two hours, three, and building up to four over a period of years.

From the start she was given special exercises to make her body supple, and was taught to understand and appreciate music, which is so important for interpretation of the floor exercise. She then learned acrobatic skills and classical dance, with an emphasis on making both appear a pleasure rather than a hard grind. The young gymnasts were given no set work on the standard competitive apparatus, like the asymmetric bars or the beam, but they were encouraged to use them, and completely familiarize themselves with the equipment. Then, when they had, there was no fear.

'At first, it was like a game,' says Nadia.

'But by the age of eight,' adds Karolyi, 'the students must be serious about gymnastics.' Was Nadia exceptional from the beginning? 'Many were,' he says. 'The important thing is that she is exceptional now.'

For Nadia, this period meant a round of monthly exams and local competitions, until at the age of ten in 1971 she was allowed to make her international debut. The competition was the Friendship Cup, a junior international tournament in Bulgaria, where she took first place on the asymmetric bars and the beam. It was certainly a promising beginning.

By 1973 she was beginning to compete against seniors. At the Rumanian International championships in Bucharest that year, against many older gymnasts from all over Europe, the twelve-year-old Nadia won all four pieces of apparatus – bars, beam, vault and floor – and of course the combined title. The same year she competed in a Friendship Tournament in East Germany, and won the asymmetric bars, the vault, and the overall title.

More and more people in gymnastics circles were beginning to talk now about this child-prodigy gymnast, already holder of the Master of Sport award in Rumania, who had been defeating so many experienced internationals in Eastern Europe. The Karolyis decided that the time was right for Nadia to stretch her wings a little more, and to compete on the other side of the Iron Curtain.

The place they chose to put Nadia under Western scrutiny for the first time was London. Or, more specifically, Wembley's Empire Pool, where the annual 'Champions All' tournament was due to be held on Saturday, 12 April 1975. Nadia's career was about to take another giant step forward.

*Chapter Four*

# CHAMPIONS ALL

'Champions All' was an international tournament, organized by the British Amateur Gymnastics Association, and which had grown in stature since its inauguration in 1971. Already it had a strong reputation, for in 1973 the elegant Russian Elvira Saadi had won the women's competition, and in 1974 she was succeeded by another Soviet gymnast, the sixteen-year-old Nina Dronova, who had earlier defeated her better known compatriots, Ludmilla Tourischeva and Olga Korbut, in a Japanese tournament.

The blond Nikolai Andrianov (later to become the outstanding male star of the Montreal Olympics) had won the men's section in 1973, and another top Soviet gymnast, Paata Shamugia, had triumphed in 1974, so the Russians were hoping to complete a hat-trick of success in both the men's and women's contests this year.

For the women's competition in 1975, they sent another highly promising schoolgirl, sixteen-year-old Ludmila Savina from Moscow, and in the days leading up to the tournament the British newspapers concentrated on Ludmila not only as the likely winner, but also as the next big star of the gymnastics world.

One paper showed a sequence of her in action, headined THE GIRL WHO CAN END OLGA'S REIGN, and another headline read RUSSIANS ARRIVE WITH NEW OLGA. In the previews, Monika Csaszar of Hungary and Gitta Escher of East Germany were named as the rivals most likely to threaten Ludmila in the tournament. No one mentioned Nadia.

But the girl about whom everyone would be talking by Saturday night was simply relaxing in her room at the Esso Hotel, a few hundred yards from the Empire Pool, and watching on television with amused curiosity some strange creatures she later called 'Vumbles'. 'They sang very nicely,' she said.

The Wombles were just one aspect of Western Europe she was seeing for the first time. The tournament was on Saturday afternoon, and 8000 people packed the famous Empire Pool, which had been the scene of the 1973 European Women's championships. Outside the huge building, fans without tickets were still hopefully looking for someone with a couple to spare. Such was the attraction of international gymnastics that even though none of the really big established names were in action, the lure of the spot and its attendant excitement was great.

The first piece of apparatus was the vault, and if any one moment could be pin-pointed as being the time that Nadia 'arrived' in Western Europe, this was it. Twelve girls were taking part in the contest, and after seven of them had vaulted, none had managed to reach a score of higher than 8·9 out of 10. Then Nadia, with two fine Tsukahara vaults, got a big reaction from the crowd, and the judges had to call a conference to discuss their marking. On this apparatus, each competitor takes two vaults with the higher mark counting, and Nadia was awarded 9·3 to take an early lead.

So suddenly this tiny girl in the white leotard, with a bandage on her right ankle and who, at thirteen, was the youngest competitor ever to take part in 'Champions All', had set the crowd alight. And the gymnast immediately to follow her on the vault was the Russian, Ludmila Savina.

Alas, it proved a disastrous start for 'the new Olga'. On her first vault she ran forward on landing, instead of taking just the one step allowed in the rules. And on her second vault, in an effort to avoid repeating the error, she leaned too far back on landing, and sat down. The judges gave her only 8·9, and at the end of the section, Nadia was leading, with Ludmila back in fourth place. Gitta Escher, the East German, had an even worse start, falling on both her vaults, and placing 12th and last on that apparatus with 8·2. Her expected challenge had already come to a premature end.

The contest moved to the asymmetric (or high and low) bars, and Savina fought back. With an agile and fluent programme, she scored 9·5, while Nadia, later to become so proficient on the bars, found them more of a problem here. Even the close attention and last-minute advice of Bela Karolyi was unable to prevent a poor climax to a good programme, and she made a mistake at the finish which forced her to improvise the ending and execute a rather uncontrolled dismount. In the warm-up she had achieved a far-more spectacular finish.

The judges still gave her 9·1, and at the halfway stage in the tournament Nadia and Ludmila Savina were dead level – 18·4 points each. To the delight of the home fans, Britain's Avril Lennox had moved into third place with 18·25.

Next came the beam, in which the gymnast has between 1 minute 15 seconds and 1 minute 35 seconds to present a programme demonstrating balance, turns, pivots, leaps, steps, acrobatics, and 'running combinations'. The beam itself is just four inches wide, and the top stands four feet off the ground, so it is rather like walking a tightrope.

Nadia's performance, which included a front aerial walkover with a half twist, showed inventiveness and daring, while many of her rivals preferred to settle for safer if less inspiring moves. It was this determination to overcome the ordinary which was to set Nadia apart. But she had not yet reached her highest stage of perfection. At one point, after two back handsprings, she almost fell, leaning right forward and back twice to regain her balance, and, as I wrote at the time, 'It was possibly only the willpower of the crowd, which had taken her to their hearts, which kept her on.'

If she had fallen, she would automatically have lost half a mark, and that, as it turned out, would have been crucial.

Nadia ended her routine with a back somersault with one and a half twists as her dismount, and her score was 9·2. Savina scored 9·15, so it seemed that with just one exercise left, the floor, Nadia had a tiny lead. In fact an appeal on Savina's behalf saw the Russian's score amended to 9·25, so as they prepared for the final activity it was Savina who now held the fractional advantage, leading 27·65 to 27·60. Avril Lennox (27·20) was still third, with hopes rising that she could gain the first-ever medal for Britain in this tournament.

And so to the floor, a 12-metres square mat on which the gymnast must perform for between one and one and a half minutes, using movements related to tumbling, acrobatics and dance. To the outsider, it looks very much like a free dance routine, especially as it is accompanied by music, but in fact a set number of requirements, such as utilization of the whole floor area, and the inclusion of at least two acrobatic series, are laid down in the Code of Points set out by the International Gymnastics Federation (F.I.G.). Judges use this code to mark, and know exactly what they're looking for, but even to those who don't, it can be an exhilarating experience to watch a world class gymnast on the floor exercise.

Nadia was to perform before her great rival, and it was vital that she did exceptionally well if she was to win, as whatever weaknesses the Russian may have had, the floor exercise was unlikely to be one of them. But it turned out that Nadia was herself playing her strongest card, with a tremendously varied and agile programme, in which she even managed to use the pauses in the music to effect.

At one point she stepped briefly outside the 12-metres area, which cost her 0·1 mark, but she was still awarded 9·7, the highest score of the day. When that mark went up on the scoreboard, the crowd for once abandoned its policy of never applauding a score while another gymnast is performing, and one of the men on the high bar must have wondered what had caused such an ovation midway through his programme!

Then came Savina, but although hers was a technically good programme it had few of the memorable passages of Nadia's performance. The Russian girl's mark, 9·45, was a good one, but Rumania had wrested the women's 'Champions All' trophy from the U.S.S.R. Nadia Comaneci had narrowly won her first tournament in the West, and in as exciting a fashion as possible.

As she stood on top of the rostrum to receive her medal and trophy, her head hardly rose above those of Savina, who was second, and Avril Lennox, who, to the delight of the British crowd, had taken the bronze medal. Above Nadia on the top step towered Lutz Mack of East Germany, who had also foiled the Russian hopes of a hat-trick by winning the men's contest, and defeating their Nikolay Nedbalsky into second place.

Result: 1, Nadia Comaneci (Rumania) 37·30; 2, Ludmila Savina (U.S.S.R.) 37·10; 3, Avril Lennox (G.B.) 36·55; 4, Gitta Escher (East Germany) 36·15; 5, Martine Audin (France) 34·90; 6. Jeannette van Ravenstijn (Holland) 34·80.

Nadia had really arrived on the international scene, and coach Bela Karolyi was pleased. 'This is her first big international challenge, and apart from a slight mistake on the bars, she did quite well,' he said afterwards. It could almost have been an understatement, for Nadia was the only gymnast to score at least 9·0 on each piece of apparatus. But not everyone was yet convinced. Some coaches said they thought that Savina had been undermarked, and that the judges were swayed by Nadia's youth and charm. They also thought that Nadia was 'a circus performer, not a classic gymnast'.

The remarks did not worry Karolyi or Nadia. They were already looking ahead to the next big test, less than a month away: the European Women's Championship, in Skien, Norway. That would perhaps decide whether Nadia was a circus performer or a gymnast.

*Chapter Five*

# EUROPEAN CHAMPION

The 1975 European Women's Gymnastics Championship were held on 3 and 4 May in the Norwegian town of Skien, which is hidden away among hills and fjords about seventy miles south-west of Oslo. As gymnasts and spectators arrived from all over Europe, there was little thought of anything other than Russian domination. Two years before, at Wembley, Ludmila Tourischeva, the overall Olympic champion of 1972, had won all five gold medals at stake in the previous European championships. Then in 1974 she had retained her own title at the World Championship in Varna. Ludmila was undisputed champion of gymnastics.

She was to have been partnered in Oslo as Russia's representatives by a girl even more well known, and herself a double gold medallist at the Munich Olympics, Olga Korbut. But Olga had been suffering from an ankle injury and did not make the journey. Her place was taken by the promising seventeen-year-old Nelli Kim, as each country was able to put two gymnasts into the event.

Before the championships began, a Norwegian journalist asked Ludmila Tourischeva why the Russians were so good. 'We train the most, that's why we're the best,' she explained simply. In that case, continued the journalist, why were the Russian *men* always beaten by the Japanese men in competition? Ludmila was accompanied by the Russian coach and former world champion Larissa Latynina, and they shared the same view: 'If our men trained as hard as our girls, they would probably be the best too.'

If there was to be any great challenge to the Russian gymnasts in Skien, most people thought it would come from the East German, Annelore Zinke; little chance was still given to Nadia. Although word of her London victory three weeks before had got around, it was dismissed in some quarters because the Russian girl she beat there, Savina, had not yet 'made it' in international circles. Promising, yes, but nowhere near as good as Tourischeva, Korbut, Kim, and Saadi, who were the really top Russians.

But in the days leading up to the championships, as more and more people saw Nadia in training, their feelings began to change. 'She went through the most unbelievable stunts,' said a local journalist, after watching her practice in the large, airy sports hall, with its curved roof, set among the woods overlooking the town. Gradually the consensus of opinion decided that perhaps Nadia did, after all, have a chance.

Nadia herself would sometimes sit watching the activity of preparation, buttoned into a large quilted anorak, and saying nothing. Outwardly, the only difference between Nadia at Wembley and at Skien was that she had changed her hairstyle from two shoulder length bunches to a pony tail. But could she reproduce her best form here, under the intense championship pressure?

On the opening day's competition, to decide the overall title, the pattern was set. In such events, the field is divided into groups, who work on different pieces of apparatus in turn. Ludmila Tourischeva, for instance, started on the asymmetric bars. But this was not to be her day.

She missed the bar with one foot on one of her moves, and momentarily her smooth and clean rhythm went astray. Then a swing to handstand did not quite reach the top, and she had to use her 'escape route' to conclude her exercise. The score of 9·35 was poor for a defending champion, and it dropped her to eighth place.

Meanwhile, Nadia had begun with the floor exercise, and her two double twists particularly caught the attention of the crowd of 5000. A mark of 9·65 set her off in the right direction, and she progressed to the vault, where her high and precise Tsukahara scored 9·7. Her routine on the bars went perfectly this time, and she was able to finish with her half-twist and back somersault dismount for a score of 9·75. Then she scored the same on the beam.

Ludmila, however, was struggling. On the beam she was only able to score 9·25, nearly falling after a free roll. She managed a respectable vault (9·5) and then turned, almost in despair, to her favourite exercise, the floor. Here, at last, for one brief minute, the crowd was treated to the Tourischeva of old. Ludmila was able to turn on a vivacious display of brilliant agility and tumbling skills, and put all her previous disasters of the day behind her.

At its conclusion, the audience rose to a great champion, having earlier been stunned by her lacklustre performances. Her floor mark of 9·8 set the spectators cheering and stamping in approval, as it was the highest mark of the championships on any piece of apparatus. But it was too late. The crowd knew it, and Ludmila knew it. She had finished fourth overall, and out of the medals today.

The crown of overall gymnastics champion of Europe went instead to the diminutive Nadia Comaneci, achieving what few had suspected was possible for one so young. Vigorously, she waved a big bunch of flowers which were presented to her along with her gold medal, atop the rostrum. The crowd rose to her.

Nelli Kim, Olga's late replacement, eased some of the Soviet disappointment by finishing second, with Annelore Zinke of East Germany third. Alina Goreac, Rumania's other representative, had finished sixth out of the thirty-nine competitors, so Rumanian gymnastics had plenty to celebrate. Alina, a twenty-three-year-old P.E. student from Bucharest, had long been one of Rumania's best gymnasts and was a medallist in the 1973 European championships, but even she must have realized that a wave of youngsters, nearly half her age and led by Nadia, would soon be all around her. Rumanian gymnastics was undergoing a metamorphosis, and this was only the beginning.

Overall result: 1, Nadia Comaneci (Rumania) 38·85; 2, Nelli Kim (U.S.S.R) 38·50; 3, Annelore Zinke (East Germany) 37·95; 4 equal, Ludmila Tourischeva (U.S.S.R) and Richarda Schmeisser (East Germany) 37·90; 6, Alina Goreac (Rumania) 37·65.

*Top* Nadia with her coach, Bela Karolyi, and his family in Rumania.
*Bottom* With her younger brother.

Performing the vault on the horse at the Montreal Olympic Games, 1976.   Mark Shearman

On the beam at the Champions All tournament at Wembley, 1975.   Alan Burrows

On the asymmetric bars at the Montreal Olympics.   Mark Shearman

During the floor exercise at the Champions All tournament at Wembley.   Alan Burrow

*Top* At home with her five Olympic medals.
*Bottom* With the Rumanian Olympic team.

Comaneci and Marta Egervari (Hungary) during a medal presentation in
Montreal.   Mark Shearman
*inset*
The Olympic results board shows maximum points — 10.0 — for Nadia Comaneci.

But of course, the European championships were by no means over. On the second day, the individual apparatus medals had to be decided, with four more titles at stake.

The leading six scorers from each piece of apparatus competed again with their new marks being added to their first-day score on that apparatus. Thus, someone who is particularly strong on, say, the vault would have an opportunity of winning a gold medal for that alone, even if she would not get close to a medal in the overall competition.

To be superb – the best in Europe – at all four pieces of apparatus, is quite remarkable, and it was that achievement which made Ludmila Tourischeva such a great champion in 1973 when she won all four individual gold medals, as well as the overall title. Ironically, the previous year at Munich she had become overall Olympic champion without actually winning on *any* individual piece of apparatus.

But in the 1975 European championships, it did not take Nadia long to underline that she was no flash in the pan. A 9·8 score in the vault won her that individual title, being added to her 9·7 of the first day for a winning total of 19·50. Then an even better routine on the asymmetric bars took her clear of Annelore Zinke, the 1974 bars World champion, to win that title. And a score of 9·75 on the beam completed a hat-trick of gold medals for Nadia in one afternoon.

A clean sweep proved just out of her grasp, as Nelli Kim (9·85) edged her for the floor exercise gold medal. Nadia (9·75) took the silver, just ahead of Ludmila Tourischeva, who was unable to recapture the brilliance of her floor routine of the previous day. She lost control of her first stream of tumbling, and went outside the 12-metres square, ending with a score of 9·55. Ludmila's solitary bronze, a sad contrast to her five golds of 1973, suggested to some that the quiet Russian might be near the end of her glittering career.

Results: Vault – 1, Nadia Comaneci (Rumania) 19·50; 2, Richarda Schmeisser (East Germany) 19·10; 3 equal, Alina Goreac (Rumania) and Nelli Kim (U.S.S.R.) 19·00; 5 equal, Ludmila Tourischeva (U.S.S.R.) and Annelore Zinke (East Germany) 18·95.

Bars – 1, Nadia Comaneci (Rumania) 19·65; 2, Annelore Zinke (East Germany) 19·55; 3, Nelli Kim (U.S.S.R.) 19·50; 4, Richarda Schmeisser (East Germany) 19·30; 5, Eva Kralova (Czech) 18·30; 6, Marta Egervari (Hungary) 17·95.

Beam – 1, Nadia Comaneci (Rumania) 19·50; 2, Nelli Kim (U.S.S.R.) 19·15; 3, Alina Goreac (Rumania) 19·00; 4, Richarda Schmeisser (East Germany) 18·85; 5, Annelore Zinke (East Germany) 18·25; 6, Eva Kralova (Czech) 17·95.

Floor – 1, Nelli Kim (U.S.S.R.) 19·55; 2, Nadia Comaneci (Rumania) 19·40; 3, Ludmila Tourischeva (U.S.S.R.) 19·35; 4, Alina Goreac (Rumania) 18·85; 5, Richarda Schmeisser (East Germany) 18·80; 6, Annelore Zinke (East Germany) 18·60.

Norwegian gymnastics journalist Lars Kolsrud summed it up as follows: 'What is the conclusion of the European Championships? Nadia Comaneci deserves all the superlatives you can find! She ended the Tourischeva era, and opened the gate for the young and fresh coming girls. In next year's Olympic Games, I believe Tourischeva will be better prepared, but I don't believe she'll be Queen any more.

'I was so sorry that Olga Korbut couldn't compete this time. She and Nadia would have met with the same weapons: high risks, stunning exercises, and a lot of charm. Well, we look forward to the Nadia/Olga battle later on, and say "Olga, you better fix that ankle of yours quick. Nadia is good, and said that she would be better in the Olympics." '

At a press conference after the championships, Ludmila Tourischeva was asked if, at the ripe old age of twenty-two, it was the end of the road for her. 'No,' she replied 'I hope to be in the Soviet team in Montreal.' In fact, her road had by no means run out; there was a return to success still ahead of her in 1975. But at that time, in Skien, it looked as if she might have been permanently replaced by Nadia, nine years her junior.

So now Nadia had become the new queen of gymnastics in an ascent to the throne so sudden that even the experts were a little bit confused about her background. One international authority got her coach mixed up with her home town, and wrote in a gymnastics magazine: 'All respect is due to her coaches, Karolyi and Gheorghe Dej . . .'

And everywhere the experts were not only admiring the courageous feats of the Rumanian, but also expressing concern as to their wisdom. 'Does Nadia really know how neckbreaking is her forward somer-sault with straddled legs from the outside support on the high bar of the asymmetric bars?' worried one. 'At Skien she swung it so high and far out that everyone was afraid she would miss the bars.' But she didn't.

The move was Nadia's version of the Radochla, a risky enough activity in its original form when invented in the 1960s by the East German gymnast Bridget Radochla. Then it involved a forward somersault from the low bar to the high bar, which was fraught with the danger of missing the higher bar and falling on to the back of the neck. But in Nadia's version, she performed it from the high bar, somersaulting and then re-grasping the same bar.

The other main talking point after Skien was how well Nadia would have fared against the injured Olga Korbut. If you accepted that Tourischeva was below her best, then where would you put Olga? She was, after all, the winner of one gold (vault) and four silver medals at the 1974 World championships in Varna, and as such could justifiably claim to be the second most-accomplished gymnast in the world, after Tourischeva.

So again, despite having won four gold and one silver medal at the European championships, Nadia was still looked upon with some suspicion by certain cynical experts. Was she really that good, or just lucky to find Tourischeva below par and Korbut injured?

As it happened, 1975 was a particularly crowded year for international gymnastics fixtures, and it seemed that the answer would be no longer coming than October, when the inaugural World Cup competition, involving the world's elite gymnasts, was to be held at the Empire Pool, Wembley.

First, however, Nadia took part in a special competition from 28 July to 1 August in a city which was eventually to mean a lot to her: Montreal. The organizers of the 1976 Olympics were staging a series of pre-Olympic competitions in many sports to try out installations and give officials some extra experience a year before the real thing. So Nadia went to Montreal with another young Rumanian gymnast, her best friend, Teodora Ungureanu, who was not only coached by Marta and Bela Karolyi as well, but rapidly becoming one of Nadia's biggest rivals.

Only Nelli Kim among the top Russians went to the Montreal contest, and Nadia won the overall competition and the asymmetric bars. Teodora was third in the points total, ahead of another Russian, Olga Koval, while Britain's Avril Lennox was 35th out of the 46 gymnasts taking part.

> Result: 1, Nadia Comaneci (Rumania) 76·85; 2, Nelli Kim (U.S.S.R.) 76·50; 3, Teodora Ungureanu (Rumania) 75·50; 4, Olga Koval (U.S.S.R.) 74·50; 5, Antonia Glebova (U.S.S.R.) 74·20; 6, Marta Egervari (Hungary) 74·05.

In late August the names were announced of the competitors chosen for the World Cup competition, in which the best twelve men and women would compete for overall and individual apparatus titles, and naturally the names of Nadia Comaneci, Ludmila Tourischeva and Olga Korbut were among them. From that moment gymnastics fans could scarcely contain their eagerness to see the long-awaited clash between

Nadia and Olga, and also to see whether Ludmila Tourischeva could recapture her form. Certainly Olga seemed to have recovered from the ankle injury which kept her out of the European championships, as in July she won the U.S.S.R. Games in Leningrad, beating Ludmila, and was promising some spectacular new elements in her programme in time for the World Cup contest.

The excitement grew. The overall women's title was due to be decided on Tuesday, 28 October, and Nadia had been drawn to perform between Ludmila and Olga on each piece of apparatus. Who was going to come out on top? Pauline Prestidge, the British women's team coach, summed up the situation: 'In technique and content, Nadia has the edge on everyone at the moment. For this World Cup, she must be favourite. She can match Korbut in everything except maturity. But none of them can match Tourischeva when she is on top form.

'There's no denying that Comaneci is brilliant. Her degree of difficulty, especially on the bars and beam, is higher than Olga's. She appears impassive before and after an exercise, though it may be that in competing against Korbut she may pick up some of that legendary sparkle to add to her own skill. Both girls have a huge advantage in their build: slim, with no wastage. It's easier for them to achieve movements of greater difficulty.'

So the gymnastics world waited impatiently. And then a couple of days before the competition was due to begin came a shock. The Rumanian delegation arrived in London without Nadia. They brought

Teodora Ungureanu and Anca Grigoras, but Nadia, they explained, was injured and would be unable to take part in the World Cup.

The competition, naturally, would go ahead, but suddenly it had been robbed of one of its main attractions. And everyone knew then that the classic confrontation would not take place until July 1976, in Montreal.

The World Cup was certainly a memorable competition in other ways, though. For a start, Ludmila Tourischeva, who was being asked a few months earlier if she had come to the end of the road, rediscovered all her old form, and performed brilliantly to take the overall title.

Olga Korbut re-injured her ankle in warming up for the floor exercise, and although she still took the silver medal in the overall contest, was unable to take part in the individual apparatus championships next day.

That virtually opened the way for Ludmila, revelling in her rediscovered best form, to take home all the gold medals – four more, for the maximum possible of five, just as she had done in the same arena two years before at the 1973 European championships.

But she had her own moment of high drama when dismounting from the asymmetric bars on the first day. As she made her final somersault off, a tension adjuster (a hook holding the wires that keep the bars upright and taut) which had gradually been straightening out unnoticed, finally gave way at the critical moment.

The whole apparatus collapsed to the ground, but fortunately Ludmila had already dismounted, and was unhurt. In fact, possessing an admirable presence of mind, she finished the exercise with her usual salute to the judges before looking over her shoulder to see what had happened. To her astonishment, there on the ground were the bars upon which she had been spinning and somersaulting, and throwing her speeding weight against, a few moments earlier.

It was frightening to consider what might have happened if the hook had given out a few seconds earlier, but once we knew she was all right, it was possible to even see an amusing side to it. After all, here was the Olympic champion showing she was back to top form by scoring a 9·8 mark and getting the apparatus to collapse as she left it, in a sort of dramatic 'follow that then!' statement. In fact, no one had to, because she was fortunately the final competitor on the bars that evening.

As Ludmila received the World Cup trophy from the hands of Princess Anne, alongside her compatriot Nikolai Andrianov, who had won the men's trophy, she was again back to her best form, and at the top of the gymnastics tree. But there was still that niggling thought about Nadia . . . what would have happened if she had been there?

One thing was certain. We would not find out that year. For 1975 was nearly over, and it only remained for Ludmila to go back home to Rostov-on-Don and train harder than ever for what she declared would be her third and final Olympic Games.

A morose Olga Korbut also had to return to the Soviet Union to prepare for the Olympics, once her ankle had mended.

And in the Rumanian town of Gheorghe Gheorghiu-

Dej, preparing for its winter snow, Nadia Comaneci could still afford to look back with satisfaction on a year in which she had proved herself to be one of the world's greatest women gymnasts. Even if she had missed the World Cup, she remained, as she celebrated her fourteenth birthday on 12 November, the youngest-ever European champion in the eighteen-year history of the event, and pre-Olympic champion.

She could look back on other successes too, such as her 'Champions All' victory in London, her win in the Rumanian national championships in her home town, in which she was awarded the first ever 10 mark in the history of the championships, and her victory in an international match against Italy, when she scored 9·95 for the floor exercise. Perfection was within reach now, surely.

The plan which had been worked out for her when she was only seven years old was beginning to bear fruit. Seven years – half of her life – had been concentrated for gymnastic excellence. Within a few months now the time would be right for the completion of the first part of that scheme – the XXI Olympic Games in Montreal.

*Chapter Six*

## INTO OLYMPIC YEAR

If the pre-Olympic year had ended on a note of some anti-climax for Nadia, after such a memorable summer, the Olympic year of 1976 began with a flourish of activity. First, though, there was a heavy spell of training, for the myth of international sport is that when a star performer is out of the public eye, he or she is doing nothing. In fact, the reverse is true. It is only when the demands of competition are over, with its attendant tiring travel and nervous build-up and let-down, that the most valuable, concentrated training can be carried out.

The tip of the iceberg which the spectator sees is the resultant performances, the glory and the acclaim. What they do not see is the endless exercises, the constant repetition, and what they do not feel is the aching muscles crying out for the salvation of some rest, or the shock and pain of an unexpected fall when trying some new and daring move. All this the international gymnast knows only too well, and it might not be an understatement to say that the 'light at the end of the tunnel' is the glory and acclaim next season, and the determination to do better. There can be no other incentive for putting oneself through such a grinding routine of training, day after day, trying to keep warm when the thermometer on the wall defies your muscles to loosen up.

For Nadia, February and March 1976 were to be months of great competitive activity. With her Rumanian teammates, she was to take part in a tour of North America, which would include a match between the U.S.A. and Rumania, and an appearance for Nadia in the brand new 'American Cup' tournament in New York.

First, though, there were some international matches in Europe in which to compete, and these found Nadia back to, and above, her best form. In a match against West Germany at Russelsheim she not only won, but scored four maximum 10·0 scores, and achieved 39·9 out of 40 for the compulsory exercises alone!

Result: 1, Nadia Comaneci (Rumania) 79·55; 2, Teodora Ungureanu (Rumania) 78·60; 3, Anca Grigoras (Rumania) 77·55; 4, Alina Goreac (Rumania) 77·05; 5, Georgeta Gabor (Rumania) 76·65; 6, Andrea Bieger (West Germany) 76·50. Teams: 1, Rumania 389·45; 2, West Germany 382·20.

In a match against the Netherlands, Nadia went better still, scoring a total of 79·8 out of a possible 80 for the combined compulsory and voluntary exercises – the highest score ever obtained in gymnastics.

Result: 1, Nadia Comaneci (Rumania) 79·80; 2, Teodora Ungureanu (Rumania) 78·95; 3, Georgeta Gabor (Rumania) 77·60; 4, Anca Grigoras (Rumania) 77·45; 5, Jeannette van Ravenstijn (Netherlands) 76·95; 6, Alina Milea (Rumania) 76·25.

Then there was a match in Bucharest between Rumania and Great Britain on 14–15 February, which would count as an Olympic qualifying competition. Not that the Rumanians were worried about qualifying for the Olympics, of course, but their opponents were. The full Rumanian squad turned out for the competition, and the British girls were very impressed with their techniques from the start of training on the day before the match. Their body tension, essential for good gymnastics, was exceptional, reported one of the visitors.

On the Saturday evening, 500 spectators watched the first part of the match, the compulsory exercises, and saw Nadia again in her best form. Her lowest mark was 9·7 on the beam, and at the end of the compulsory section she led easily (39·35) from her teammate Teodora Ungureanu (38·60), with Avril Lennox being the best of the British girls, lying fifth (37·70).

Next day over a thousand spectators gathered to watch the voluntary exercises, which started at 10.30 in the morning. Nadia began with a calmly-executed Tsukahara vault, which earned 9·9 from the judges, and then moved on to the asymmetric bars. Here the whole Rumanian team's warm-up exercises were so good that they earned spontaneous applause from the crowd, and in the competition itself Nadia again demonstrated her Radochla move on the high bar, drawing a gasp from the crowd. Another 9·9.

Then disaster on the beam. After a good start, Nadia missed her footing on a free cartwheel, and fell off. It was a rare moment in her international career, but she remounted and finished unperturbed with a perfect double cartwheel and twisting back somersault to dismount. She lost 0·5 of a mark automatically for falling from the beam, but still managed 9·3, and concluded her competition with a 9·8 score for the floor exercise.

There was no question as to who had won overall, but it was interesting to see the continued improvement of Ungureanu, who had managed now to elevate herself to the position of Nadia's permanent shadow.

The Rumanians took six of the first seven places, with only Avril Lennox (fifth) able to get in amongst them.

Rumania, naturally, won the match, but the British team and officials were still elated. They had managed to obtain 36 separate scores of 9·0 and above in the match, and all six British girls had reached the qualifying scores for the Olympics. Unfortunately, later in the year, the qualifying conditions for Montreal were altered controversially, but at this time the British squad were radiantly happy, and unabashed at the gap in standard between the two teams.

The difference in approach to the match was underlined by one of the British gymnasts who said: 'The Rumanians seemed to be treating it like a mere training session, working hard and repeating many individual moves. After the competition was over we were amazed to see that they didn't even leave the gymnasium. They simply piled a few large sponges under the bars, and carried on training'. For Nadia and her companions, this match was just one more step towards Montreal.

Result: 1, Nadia Comaneci (Rumania) 78·25; 2, Teodora Ungureanu (Rumania) 77·50; 3, Anca

Grigoras (Rumania) 75·65; 4, Alina Goreac (Rumania) 75·65; 5, Avril Lennox (G.B.) 75·35; 6, Georgeta Gabor (Rumania) 74·70. Teams: 1, Rumania 383·20; 2, Gt Britain 367·55.

And so then it was off to North America, with Canada as the first stop. In a Toronto competition, Nadia really began to shine, scoring ten out of ten six times from a possible maximum of eight. Only very rarely is even one ten awarded to a gymnast in a competition, let alone six.

But it was a situation which once again raised doubts from the cynics, who said that it was impossible, that the scores must have been inflated out of all proportion, and that the Canadians must have been taken in by the difference between their own gymnastics standard and that of Eastern Europe. But they were soon to find out that Nadia was a gymnast with a unique talent for perfection.

Next the Rumanian squad flew to Tucson, Arizona, for their international match on 27–28 February with the U.S.A., which would also count as an Olympic qualifying contest. Held at the University of Arizona's McKale Centre, it was watched by an excited crowd of more than 6500. Both Nadia and Teodora scored exactly the same total marks as they had done against Great Britain, 78·25 and 77·50, but found the Americans tougher opposition. Kathy Howard of the U.S. finished second to Nadia on the floor exercise, and Debbie Willcox finished second to Nadia on the asymmetric bars. Nadia won the overall contest, and individually the floor, vault and bars, but in the beam

46

she again fell off, and both Teodora Ungureanu and Anca Grigoras beat her, with Nadia tying for third place with American Tammy Manville. Rumania won the match, but the U.S.A. had some consolation in a men's match held at the same time in Berkeley, California, in which the U.S.A. beat Rumania by 568·75 to 564·60.

Results: 1, Nadia Comaneci (Rumania) 78·25; 2, Teodora Ungureanu (Rumania) 77·50; 3, Debbie Willcox (U.S.) 76·15; 4, Kathy Howard (U.S.) 75·80; 5, Ann Carr (U.S.) 75·65; 6, Alina Goreac (Rumania) 75·50. Teams: 1, Rumania 381·10; 2, U.S.A. 379.20.

U.S. Olympic team manager Rod Hill reported afterwards in the magazine *International Gymnast*:

'There are not enough words to explain the tremendous impact a gymnast such as Nadia Comaneci has on the sport. A week before arriving in Arizona, the youngster scored a perfect ten in six of the eight events she competed in (Toronto). Many yelled it is impossible, the scores were raised, and so on. Before their tour of the U.S.A. was over, it was obvious that it *is* possible. This youngster does not make many mistakes. Two years ago I took my Denver School of Gymnastics team to Rumania, and we were the first people from the Free World to see this superstar. I reported in this magazine at the time that I had just seen the greatest gymnast the world has ever seen and would see for some time. My comments were met with some laughter. Those who laughed are not laughing now. She has come and they have seen.

'Nadia is in a class all her own. She is the best, and she knows it. She admits she is worried about no other gymnasts in the world, except her own teammates. She is perfection in motion. She could throw ten, twenty or thirty routines and score 9·8 or better in each of them. I have seen her throw six consecutive bar routines and hit every one of them, and not be breathing hard. Her physical condition is fantastic. Teodora is not far behind, and in fact has beaten Nadia, which no one else can claim. Also, there are others back home from the same club who will be on the Olympic team, replacing those we saw here.'

Hill was also intrigued by the diet of the Rumanians. 'When we went to dinners together (in Tucson), nobody saw Nadia, Teodora or Georgeta Gabor (who are all gymnasts under Bela Karolyi, the Rumanian coach) eat a bite of food. I was with them a week, and saw them eat but a small portion of chicken. What they eat I am not sure of, but I have reason to believe it is vitamin supplements. Every girl on the Rumanian team was slim and hard. By the time four months are up, they will be trained to a fine competitive edge. The American girls do not show this conditioning. In some cases we had overweight girls on the floor, and this was confirmed by Madama Valerie Nagy of Hungary, who was there to oversee the scores. If we hope to stay close in Montreal, we too have to train and hone these girls to a fine edge.'

From Tucson, the Rumanian squad went on first to Albuquerque, then to San Francisco and Denver. At each city, Nadia won the competition and wowed not only the American gymnasts and coaches, but also those among the American public who couldn't tell a vaulting horse from a balance beam.

But the travelling and competitions gradually wore down the frail Nadia, and she developed flu symptoms. The party returned home to Rumania, and then after four days rest to try to banish the germs, she returned to the U.S.A. for the 'American Cup' competition in New York on 27–28 March. This was a brand new tournament, inaugurated to celebrate the 200th anniversary of American independence, and staged by the United States Gymnastics Federation at the world famous Madison Square Garden.

The competition called for one male and one female gymnast from each country, and Nadia was accompanied by the muscular twenty-five-year-old Rumanian men's champion, Dan Grecu. Altogether eleven countries were represented, including the Soviet Union, who sent their own tiny fourteen-year-old, Yelena Davidova, to compete against Nadia.

In both the men's and women's competitions, all the gymnasts took part in the Saturday events, and the leading six then continued, but with a clean score sheet, in the finals on the second day, Sunday.

A crowd of more than 10,000 packed Madison Square Garden, and Nadia immediately captured them by performing her perfectly piked Tsukahara vault for a ten score in the opening event. (Ironically, the inventor of the vault, Japan's Mitsuo Tsukahara, was competing in the men's competition, and scored only 9·5 for his version!) With 9·85 on the bars, 9·8 for the beam and 9·75 for the floor exercise, Nadia easily led the qualifiers for the final next day with 39·40 out of 40. She had almost two full marks to spare over Kathy Howard (U.S.A.), who had 37·45, and Yelena Davidova of the Soviet Union, who was third with 37·20.

In the finals, Nadia simply swamped the opposition with her class. She received 9·85 from the judges on her vault – and that was her *worst* mark! Her bars routine got 9·9, her beam exercise (she stayed on this time) 9·95, and the floor another ten. No one else was near her. Kathy Howard, a late substitute for the injured Pan-American Games champion Ann Carr, rose well to the occasion, finishing second, but her score of 38·15 was far behind Nadia's 39·70. Davidova was third (36·85).

If the American public had needed any further proof of Nadia's excellence, they now had it. And as their male gymnast, the blond Bart Conner, had won the men's trophy (with Nadia's compatriot Dan Grecu in third place), they did not begrudge the little Rumanian her spirited victory. They were spellbound by her brilliance, and puzzled by her lack of emotion. Unlike Olga Korbut, who was always a favourite when she appeared in the U.S.A., Nadia did not wave and smile to the crowd, and never seemed to lap up their attention in the same way.

'It is not her nature to smile,' explained a Rumanian official to the wondering American journalists, and Bela Karolyi added: 'It is her character to be serious.'

Later, though, she did let a smile across her face when she stood, clutching her giant trophy and a bouquet of flowers, at the presentation ceremony. The men's winner, Bart Conner, gave her a kiss on the cheek for the benefit of the photographers, and he and Nadia stood side by side holding their identical trophies aloft as the crowd gave them a huge ovation.

> Result: 1, Nadia Comaneci (Rumania) 39·70; 2,
> Kathy Howard (U.S.) 38·15; 3, Yelena Davidova
> (U.S.S.R.) 36·85; 4 equal, Zsuzsa Nagy (Hungary)
> and Reiko Yoshida (Japan) 36·55; 6, Silvia Anjos
> (Brazil) 34·45.

Afterwards, Nadia was interviewed on American
television, and the conversation, in English, went like
this:

'How are you, Nadia?'

'Yes, I'm fine.'

'Are you looking forward to the Olympics?'

'I want for myself gold medal.'

'How many?'

'Five.'

'Does it bother you to be constantly compared to
Olga Korbut?'

'I'm not Olga Korbut. I'm Nadia Comaneci.'

Despite her limited English, Nadia realized the name
of Olga Korbut was one which would keep recurring
everywhere she went. Not only were the two girls
equally brilliant gymnasts, causing vast interest in
what would happen when they finally met head-on,
but also because to many people Olga Korbut was the
only other gymnast in the world of whom they had
ever heard.

The Rumanian squad had several international
matches still to contest as Spring approached, but
Nadia was suffering from an elbow injury (not sur-
prisingly, as someone worked out that she had competed in fourteen tournaments within a few weeks!) So

she missed the Rumanian national championships, and also the matches against France and North Korea.

In the French match Teodora Ungureanu stepped up to victory with 77·60 points, from team-mates Gabor and Grigoras, with Rumania winning the match by 378·55 to 369·35. And against North Korea, Teodora was herself missing, leaving Grigoras the winner with 78·85, and Rumania taking the overall contest by 389·25 to 385·40. Such high scores, incidentally, incurred the wrath of many international experts, who felt they were being 'pumped up' to reach Olympic qualifying levels; it was largely this sort of reaction which eventually led to the change in qualifying conditions for Montreal.

Teodora Ungureanu, meanwhile, was following in her close friend's footsteps by travelling to Wembley's Empire Pool to defend for her country, coach, and indeed home town of Gheorghe Gheorghiu-Dej, the 'Champions All' title won by Nadia twelve months earlier.

A large photograph of Nadia adorned the front page of the programme for the tournament, held on 10 April 1976, and the contest was still growing in importance. This time the U.S.A. was to be represented for the first time, by seventeen-year-old Los Angeles student Denise Cheshire, while the U.S.S.R. sent this year a sixteen-year-old Minsk schoolgirl, Lidia Gorbik.

Teodora had been to Wembley once before, to the World Cup six months earlier, but this time she made far more impact. She led after the first event, the vault, with a high, half-piked Tsukahara which earned her 9·5, and followed that up with a good bars performance

(9·65), although the American girl was even better (9·7).

Gorbik had a poor bars exercise, but made up for it somewhat by scoring 9·7 on the beam, where Teodora only received 9·5. But at one point the Rumanian amazed the crowd by doing two complete rotations on the beam while in a splits-handstand position.

With only the floor exercise left, Teodora led the field comfortably and put the issue beyond doubt by scoring a remarkable 9·9, the highest mark ever seen in Britain. At one point during her performance she executed a splits leap to catch hold of her own ankle and then go straight into a dive roll.

Her personality, too, attracted a lot of comment: more vivacious, people said. She was not like the robot she had been the previous October. Small wonder then that when Nadia was asked later in the year who she considered her greatest danger in Montreal she named neither a Russian nor an East German, but Teodora Ungureanu.

*Chapter Seven*

## MONTREAL PREPARATIONS

For most of the world's gymnasts, the next two
months was a time for a return to the gymnasium to
finish polishing the routines which would be on show
at the Montreal Olympics in July.

Meanwhile, in Montreal itself, the final preparations
were under way for the staging of the XXI Olympic
Games, and the myriad of problems which that entailed.
Doubts linger over whether the huge Olympic Stadium,
centrepiece of the Opening and Closing Ceremonies
and all the athletics events, would be ready in time.
The International Press Centre, planned to be situated
in the Stadium's Tower, had already been moved into
the centre of the city of Montreal when it was realized
that the Tower would not be built in time for the
Games. And thousands of security troops and police
moved into the city at an estimated cost of £70 million,
in an effort to prevent any recurrence of the 1972
Munich tragedy in which terrorists broke into the
Israeli quarters in the Olympic Village and brought
death and bloodshed to the Games.

But the delay in building the Stadium, caused by a
series of strikes among the construction workers,
threatened to disrupt the gymnastics programme only
in the sense that at one point it was feared that the
whole Games might have to be delayed, or even moved

elsewhere. For the gymnastics competition was a somewhat self-contained unit, due to take place at the Montreal Forum, an already well-established building in the heart of the city, whereas some of the other sports were relying on newly-completed or partially completed facilities.

Even the last-minute walkout from the Games by a number of African countries, who refused to compete unless New Zealand (who had sent a rugby union team to tour South Africa) withdrew, did not affect the gymnastics programme, dominated by Europeans, Americans and the Japanese.

The Montreal Forum had been built in 1924, and was even larger than the Empire Pool, Wembley. It was about six miles from the Olympic Village, and even had an address on the main road – 2313 St Catherine Street West – where it stood opposite a busy square which serves as an intersection to the bus and underground railway routes.

The building, which seats 16,400 people, had been entirely renovated in 1968 and equipped with an air-conditioning system. Normally, it was the scene of ice-hockey, and was the home base of the famous Montreal Canadiens team, but during the Olympics it was going to house not only the gymnastics, but also later on some finals of the basketball, boxing and volleyball.

Some of the newer Olympic buildings were set in more inspiring surroundings, with open courtyards and long approach roads, but the Forum nevertheless had a character all of its own, nestling up against a parade of shops, cinemas and hamburger bars. And anyway it is not the facilities which make an Olympic

55

Games: it is the people who use them.

From early in July, thousands of them, together with officials, coaches and other members of national team delegations, arrived in Montreal, and moved into the huge Olympic Village, which consisted of four separate nineteen-storey apartment blocks designed to resemble a pair of giant pyramids.

Three of the blocks housed the male competitors and officials, and the fourth one the females. It was here that Nadia and her teammates would live, eat, sleep and for the first time experience the unique atmosphere generated by this gathering of the world's greatest sportsmen and women, all awaiting the moment when their chance would come to put their years of training to the test.

Altogether 11,000 competitors and officials were housed in the Olympic Village, and guarded by a huge security net. To get in and out of the Village, for instance, Nadia had to show a special competitor's pass with her photograph on it, at two separate entrances as well as in the tower block itself. Armed guards patrolled the edge of the Village grounds, inside tall wire fences, while on the grass a few feet behind them the sportsmen of the world tried to put the tensions out of their minds by throwing frisbees to each other, or playing soccer with piles of tracksuits as the goalposts.

As Nadia and her teammates explored the rabbit-warren corridors of the Village, they found shops, a library, cinema, television rooms, lounges, swimming pools, restaurants, a bank, sauna bath, and boutiques. Most of these were situated in a part known as the International Centre, where they could meet up with friends and visitors who were not staying in the Village but who, armed with the right form supplied by a national team delegation, could enter that part of the Village for a limited time during the day.

The International Centre was actually a school, converted for the duration of the Games into part of the Village complex, and in what was normally the school playground, dozens of tables with sunshades were set out in front of a stage as a social centre. At regular intervals dancers, musicians, conjurors and other entertainers would put on a 'live' show to amuse the competitors and their friends, who could sit at the tables with a drink and a sandwich and relax.

In the basement of one of the huge tower blocks was the international cafeteria, which was open twenty-four hours a day and prided itself on being able to supply a vast array of international dishes to please all tastes. As everything was free to Village residents (daily visitors were not allowed in here) of course there was always the danger that a competitor was going to take too much food and spoil their chances in the Games. The gymnasts particularly had to overcome this temptation, which would have made more difference to them than to a weightlifter or shot putter.

All the time, though, there was a reminder amid the friendly inter-mingling of the competitors of the security measures. Police and troops were always circling any area where a lot of people gathered, just to keep an eye on things, and every time anybody went into the Village they had to have their briefcase, holdall or handbag searched, had to pass through a metal-detector frame, and sometimes undergo a body search with a hand-held metal detector which would screech if it came upon even a bunch of keys in your pocket. However many times you went in or out, you were always searched.

Despite the social activities, it was a taut, tense place to live, even for a couple of weeks, and the more you moved about the more you became aware of the tight security which never eased until the Games were over. Many of the competitors confined themselves to just socializing in the Common Room, situated on each floor in the residential blocks. It was really just an open terrace, but had been equipped with television sets, stereo record players and radios, newspapers and magazines. And there was always time for writing letters home, or the great joy of actually getting a letter *from* home. Then the competitors had to remind themselves just why they were there in that giant 'hotel', and how much interest from so many millions of people around the world was being focused on the Quebec city of Montreal.

Montreal had been awarded the 1976 Olympic Games in May 1970, after nearly forty years of trying to win the confidence of the International Olympic Committee. Indeed, because Montreal was visited in 1889 by the Frenchman, Baron Pierre de Coubertin, founder of the Modern Olympic Games, seven years before the first Modern Games were held in 1896, many people feel that it was discovering how important amateur sport was in the daily lives of the Canadians that encouraged him to pursue his venture.

By the 1970s the Games had reached such gigantic proportions, however, that the question is now being asked frequently as to whether they have become too big. Some people think that a breaking up of the Games, with its twenty-odd sports, is inevitable, with different cities, or even different countries, each staging a few.

The gymnastics programme, for instance, has grown enormously. In 1928 women gymnasts took part in the Olympics for the first time, with the Dutch winning the team prize, but in 1932 there were so few entries for the women's events that they were not held. They were revived in 1936 at Berlin, and by the 1950s and 1960s some of the greatest ever gymnasts were being seen, and legends born.

The superb Russian star Larissa Latynina, overall Olympic champion in 1956 and 1960, won a total of nine gold, five silver and four bronze medals in three Olympic appearances (a figure unsurpassed by any competitor in any other Games sport), while the Czech girl Vera Caslavska, the overall champion in 1964 and 1968, won seven gold and four silvers in her Olympic career from 1960–68.

Both these ladies would be leading figures in their national team delegations at Montreal, and with gymnastics having really stirred the public imagination through Olga Korbut's performances at Munich in 1972, interest in the sport at Montreal was certain to be vast. At the Forum, space was reserved for no less than 740 journalists, representing worldwide news and television services.

And so the world's best gymnasts began settling in at the Olympic Village. Nadia had as her teammates some of her friends from home, including Teodora Ungureanu, while Anca Grigoras, Mariana Constantin,

Gabriela Trusca and Georgeta Gabor made up the rest of the Rumanian squad. Nadia and Teodora had missed a recent match against Hungary, through slight injury, but had returned to show their top form in a trial event before leaving Rumania. Nadia scored 79·75 out of 80, and Teodora 78·70.

The youngsters were dominating, and even the experienced Alina Goreac did not gain selection for the Rumanian squad, which had an average age of just fifteen-and-a-half! Apart from Gabor, who was two months younger, Nadia was the 'baby' of the team, in terms of age if not standard, while Grigoras and Trusca were, at eighteen, the 'grannies'. They were also the only two of the six not coached by Marta and Bela Karolyi, so it was clear that the youth policy was working.

The Soviet Union had also been deciding on its Olympic team composition at their national championship, which was won, not by Olga Korbut nor Ludmila Tourischeva, but by Nelli Kim. She scored 77·20 to defeat Elvira Saadi (76·65) and Tourischeva (who made a mistake on the bars and scored 76·60). Olga Korbut, who messed up her routine on the beam, was fourth with 76·45, while Lidia Gorbik and Svetlana Grozdova completed the six. In Montreal their seventh girl, the tiny fifteen-year-old Maria Filatova, was finally included instead of Gorbik, but even so this still gave the team an average age of nineteen-and-a-half, or an advantage of four years experience per gymnast over the Rumanians. So it was clear that if that was to count for much, the Soviet Union would be unlikely to lose the women's team title which they had held since

1952 . . . long before any of the Rumanian girls were born.

Russian coach Larissa Latynina said: 'I feel that Nelli Kim has a good chance against Comaneci.' Nelli herself added: 'To compete successfully with Nadia it will be necessary to enrich the exercises with original and complicated movements. Her exercises include many of them, and she performs them easily and without apparent effort.' Which, being paraphrased, meant in effect that she thought it was going to be damned hard to beat Nadia.

The eighteen-year-old Nelli, with her attractive features, came from the Kazakh city of Chimkent, 1500 miles south-east of Moscow, and did seem to be the girl who could challenge Nadia more closely than either Ludmila Tourischeva or Olga Korbut. But now there was little point in speculating: everyone just had to wait and see.

The Games were not due to open officially until Saturday 17 July, and the gymnastics would be getting under way with the women's set exercises from 8.30 the next morning. But to give the gymnasts a chance to try out the apparatus at the Forum, special rehearsal sessions, open to the public, were held a few days beforehand. Until then the gymnasts had been training at various schools within a few miles of the Olympic Village, and they all welcomed the chance to perform on the real thing in the Forum.

These sessions were not to be marked, but each country would formally march in and spend a certain amount of time on all four pieces of apparatus, while the announcer would keep reminding the audience that the names and marks shown on the scoreboard were entirely fictitious and did not relate to anything actually happening in the arena. They were simply testing the scoring devices.

On Tuesday 13 July the Rumanian and Russian gymnasts found themselves in the Montreal Olympic arena together for the first time, and completely put the Hungarian and East German teams, appearing simultaneously, into the shade as their gymnasts vied for the crowd's attention in a calm piece of pre-Gamesmanship.

Nadia and Teodora both drew big applause for their high vaulting, but one of the hits of the evening was the little Russian, Maria Filatova, just 4ft 5¾ins in height and weighing 4st 10lbs, and who made even the 5ft Olga Korbut look tall. The 14,000 crowd, paying a dollar each to watch, thought she was sweet if not as accomplished as her rivals.

Olga herself, with a bandage on her right ankle, had an unhappy evening, falling from the beam and hurting her right arm. Nelli Kim also fell from the beam, but it didn't matter – yet.

For the gymnastic fans, the actual sight of Nadia Comaneci and Olga Korbut in the same arena together at last was one to relish. It had not happened at the 1975 European championships, and it had not happened at the 1975 World Cup.

But now these two girls – one the biggest name in gymnastics, the other her potential successor – were shortly going to meet in competition for the first time ever. No one meant to take anything away from the pleasant and technically brilliant Ludmila Tourischeva

62

and Nelli Kim, but for many spectators, both in Montreal and watching on television around the world, there were only two gymnasts in the 1976 Olympic tournament: Olga and Nadia.

## Chapter Eight

# PERFECTION

The Olympic Games began with the classic Opening Ceremony in the main stadium on Saturday 17 July, with the march past of all the competing nations, the taking of the Olympic Oath of amateurism, and the lighting of the Olympic Flame. At least gymnastics competitors and fans would not have to wait long for their competitions to begin.

It was only the next day, Sunday, when the events got underway in the Forum, with its steep banked seating and orange floor-exercise matting, which dominated the area. The first competition to be decided would be the team contest, spread over two days, Sunday and Monday. On the first day the gymnasts would perform the compulsory exercises on each piece of apparatus, and on the second the voluntary exercises.

With a total of eighty-seven gymnasts in this competition, however, it would take a long time to get through, even with the competitors working in four simultaneous groups. The judges, of course, had to have breaks, while at the same time trying to ensure that they were applying the same standards for those who performed at 8.30 in the morning as they were for those who would not be on until six o'clock in the evening. Four separate sessions were needed on both days, and it took until 4.45 p.m. on the Sunday before the leading countries, including Rumania and the Soviet Union, came on to the floor for the first time. The Russians, the defending team Olympic champions, were to perform first on the asymmetric bars, while the Rumanians had been assigned to the beam.

Gymnasts particularly dislike having to start on the beam because it makes such great demands not only acrobatically but also in terms of balance, and it is often difficult to do well until completely attuned to the surroundings and the occasion. However, dressed identically in their smart white tracksuits with the Rumanian national colours splashed across the front, and the single word, ROMANIA over the left breast of the jacket, Nadia and her colleagues began their stretching and warming up, watched by Marta Karolyi.

At the opposite end of the arena, the Russian team with their coach, Larissa Latynina, were preparing for the asymmetric bars. For many people it would be the first time they had seen Ludmila Tourischeva work on the bars since that dramatic and potentially lethal moment at the Wembley World Cup the previous October when the whole apparatus had collapsed after her dismount. But her nerve, obviously, had not suffered. She scored 9·75, but Nelli Kim earned 9·8, and then – back into her best form at the right time – Olga Korbut, displaying all her old agility and style, impressed the judges sufficiently for them to award 9·9.

Because the asymmetric bars exercise takes less than half the time of the beam, the whole Russian squad had finished before Nadia had started her first exercise. Teodora Ungureanu had just scored 9·75 as the Russians sat down in a line on the team bench and waited for the signal to move to their next piece of apparatus. So they saw every moment of Nadia's performance on the beam, as she was the last of the Rumanian team to work. Cameras whirred and flashlights exploded as she went through her beam routine flawlessly.

At one point she lifted herself into a handstand position so slowly that it seemed she could surely not have enough momentum, or strength in that skinny little body, to get to the full vertical position as she swung her legs overhead. But she was in complete control, and just stressing the fact. At the end of the exercise, the audience response was thunderous and as the Russian team went to pick up their bags they heard a second wave of enthusiasm enveloping the arena. Nadia had scored 9·9, exactly the same as Olga on the bars!

This seemed as if it was going to be a confrontation in a million, not only because of the high scoring, but also because Nadia ran back on to the arena to wave to the crowd. It was a telling moment for those who had complained that she was so often sullen and unsmiling. Instead of letting everything waft over her head, as she had done in previous major contests, this time she was apparently going to take on Olga in all fields, including flirtation with the spectators.

The Russians moved next to the beam, where the difference in standard on this apparatus was quickly apparent. It was not a huge difference, because the girls here were the finest in the world and the defects minimal. But both Kim and Tourischeva, scoring 9·4, swayed slightly; Olga Korbut did not, but received 'only' 9·8. Tourischeva came into her own on the floor, scoring 9·9 for a fluid and agile display, while Nadia received 9·75 for the floor and 9·7 for her vault.

Then it was on to the asymmetric bars for the Rumanians. Here the teamwork of Nadia and Teodora was always at its most apparent, because one would always clamber up on to the lower bar to rub down the higher bar for her friend when she was due to perform, while the other would be chalking up her hands. And then after the performance they would swap responsibility. Teodora went first and scored a stunning 9·9 to confirm her rise in stature, and then it was Nadia's turn. Working with absolutely the right amount of control and flair, she drew a gasp from the crowd with the daring of her routine, and landed to a burst of acclaim. Even the other gymnasts were clapping.

Everyone watched the scoreboard beside the bars. A wait, and then the figures which were to make Olympic history. 10·0! Nadia Comaneci had become the first gymnast in the history of the Olympic Games to score a perfect ten. She was the first gymnast who, watched by thousands in the arena, countless hundreds of millions at home, and under the greatest pressure possible in sport, had turned in a performance with which the judges could find no fault.

She waved again to the crowd, and the crowd waved back. The Russian gymnasts were looking at each other, and the Russian coach Larissa Latynina later protested that it could not be perfect because Nadia appeared to take two steps on landing, instead of one. But the score was not altered.

'I knew it was faultless,' said Nadia afterwards,

'because I have done it sixteen times before.'

The one consolation the Russians had as they climbed into the buses which would take them back to the Olympic Village was that overnight they were leading the team competition collectively by 194·20 to Rumania's 192·70, and it did not seem likely that they could be beaten. But Nadia Comaneci was obviously in the sort of form they feared for the individual events.

Taken completely by surprise, though, was the Olympic Organizing Committee's results computer. 'Because of that little girl's perfect score, four computer experts will be working through the night to revise the computer programme so that a perfect score can be accommodated,' said a results official.

He explained that when the computer programme was designed with the advice of experts six months earlier, the technicians were told that a perfect score was an impossibility. Now the whole thing would have to be revised. 'We're not necessarily expecting another perfect score, but just in case, we'll be ready,' he added.

Their time spent adjusting the computer would not be wasted.

Meanwhile headlines like NADIA STUMPS RESULTS SYSTEM were appearing all over the world. The first perfect gymnast? Everyone wanted to see her, so the success of the rest of the programme was guaranteed.

Next day the second half of the team competition started at 2 p.m., building slowly up to a climax, so that by the start of the fourth group of teams, including the Russians and the Rumanians, at 8.15 that evening, the whole atmosphere in the Forum was electric.

As the teams marched in, eyes were straining to spot Nadia among the six young Rumanians. She was still unknown by sight to many spectators, and indeed to some journalists who had not been present on Sunday and who had been sent rushing by their papers to the Forum after the previous day's happenings.

It was always difficult to spot Nadia among her teammates if you didn't know her, because they all looked so alike, whereas spotting Olga Korbut among the Russians was, of course, very easy for anyone with even the vaguest knowledge of gymnastics. For some people that Monday night the key to identification of Nadia was simply the number 73 on her back. By the end of the week, though, they would recognize her well enough, with her pony tail tied with ribbons in the Rumanian national colours, and her cheerful waving and smiling to the crowd (such a vivid contrast to last year).

The session opened with Tourischeva performing well on the bars to score 9·8, followed by Olga Korbut repeating her 9·9. But Nadia was improving on her beam work of the previous day, and there on the scoreboard was something which must have gladdened the hearts of the men who had sat up all night adjusting the computer scoring system, if no one else: 10·0. Nadia had done it again. At the other end of the arena, Olga looked over her shoulder to see what the roar was about, and looked away again.

The gymnasts moved round. Tourischeva was awarded 9·85 for her beam work, a mark matched by Olga, but which she could have improved if she had not momentarily lost control and had to wave her arms around to regain balance. It was a good exercise otherwise, but Nadia was competing for the spectators' attention as she simultaneously went through her floor exercise. She was also given 9·85.

Olga moved on to the floor exercise herself, but while warming up with a double back somersault her foot seemed to go from under her and she suddenly stumbled awkwardly on to the mat. She stood up and prodded the area with her toe, as if looking for some defect, but if it was there, real or imaginary, she found it again on the actual exercise, stumbled again, and her mark dropped down to 9·7.

At the precise moment Olga finished her floor routine, Nadia executed her Tsukahara vault (9·85) and you simply could not tell for which girl the crowd was cheering most. But it was loud. 'I haven't heard the old place rock like this even when the Montreal Canadiens have scored a winning goal in the last seconds,' said one veteran Canadian reporter.

Ludmila Tourischeva managed to almost equal the reception with an immaculate floor exercise, which scored 9·95, and it was strange to recall that only a year or so before people were actually asking whether, after her defeat in the European championships, she had come to the end of the road.

So to the final change round of apparatus, and by now it was clear that only if the entire Russian team collapsed into a quivering heap, unable to move, would they lose the team title. But they didn't. Instead, they added more points to their score, with a 9·9 vault from Nelli Kim, and the same for the prodigous Maria Filatova. Olga Korbut was less happy as her re-injured ankle let her down somewhat on her vaulting, and she sat down heavily on one of her two attempts. But she managed a 9·7 with the other vault, and the team title was now beyond any other country's reach.

There was still Nadia to perform on the asymmetric bars, however, and it may not have been a coincidence that Olga chose this moment to limp over somewhat ostentatiously to a water dispenser, with her back to the bars, to pour out some water to put on her ankle. She has been such a marvellous asset to the sport of gymnastics at and since the Munich Olympics that it is always sad to see her in this mood, a kind of jealous frustration. She reacted the same way at the World Cup the previous autumn when, prevented from competing because of a similar ankle injury, she went out of the arena, unable to watch Ludmila Tourischeva cleaning up the gold medals. I saw her then alone under the main stand at Wembley, unhappily eating an endless round of hotdogs and sandwiches for which she wasn't really hungry, but simply using to try to ease her misery.

Anyway, her reaction here was sad but understandable. The big confrontation with Nadia had been so long in coming, she had started so well, and now her suspect ankle had let her down again. Not only was she in danger of losing medals to the young Rumanian, she was also (worse, perhaps, for Olga) losing the crowd. A lot would depend on how quickly the Soviet doctors could patch up her ankle to let her continue later in the week in the individual competitions.

On the bars, meanwhile, Nadia was again perfect and again the roof almost came off the Forum when her mark was put on the scoreboard. Another ten. That made three maximum scores in two days, and it could no longer be considered as merely luck. The girl was brilliant.

'Nadia simply outclasses everyone,' said Carol Ann Letheren, technical chairman of the Canadian Gymnastics Federation afterwards. 'She's an incredible performer. She just doesn't break.'

When the teams went on to the medal rostrum at the end of the evening, the winning Russian team received a huge ovation, but a renewed wave of applause and cheering greeted the Rumanians as they stepped up to receive their silver medals. Nadia waved again to the crowd, and then Olga leaned over and shook hands with her. Nadia said later: 'I feel we are friends.'

Result: 1, U.S.S.R. 390·35; 2, Rumania 387·15; 3, East Germany 385·10; 4, Hungary 380·15; 5, Czechoslovakia 378·25; 6, U.S.A. 375·05.

For the first time, Nadia met the world's press in a hectic late night news conference, and the grinning, waving girl she had become in the arena over the past two days reverted to being the quiet, solemn and rather shy girl of the past. She said she was 'glad' to have got three maximum scores, but was not concerned about finding something else for which to strive. 'I shall try to surpass myself, to do better than I did before,' she added, gravely.

'If she wants to do that,' said one journalist to another, 'they'll have to invent a new sport.'

She was asked about her family back in Gheorghe Gheorghiu-Dej, who hadn't been able to come to

Montreal, but would be watching it all on television at home, and also about her three-to-four hours a day training. She was even asked about her diet, and she told journalists how she had eaten ham, eggs and milk for breakfast, with soup, steak and fruit for lunch.

Someone asked if she had a boy friend. 'I do have friends, and some of them are boys,' answered Nadia through an interpreter, leaving the confused reporters looking at each other and wondering whether that answer meant yes or no.

Then she was asked about the qualities which make a good gymnast. 'Courage, perseverance, hard work and, of course, grace,' she said.

Which one of her rivals did she fear the most? One of the Russians perhaps? No, she said, Teodora Ungureanu was her biggest rival. How do you spell that? they asked.

The Russian team had now arrived at the press conference, and they took up a place in the opposite corner of the room, waiting for their turn, and sipping lemonade. Olga was limping, and holding a towel with ice in it, which she immediately placed over her ankle when she sat down.

Eventually, the press had finished with the Rumanian team, or rather with Nadia, to whom most of the questions had been directed, and she was able to get away, back to the Olympic Village. Being surrounded by so many strange faces, with people leaning into her, trying to catch every word she uttered in her piping voice, poking microphones and camera lenses at her, was all very unnerving. It was far worse, she admitted, than being in the arena, performing, but she left the conference with a message in French, the widely spoken language in Montreal, and one of her best subjects at school: 'Je remercie beaucoup la publique Canadienne.'

As the attention turned to the Soviet team, Larissa Latynina, their coach, who had been critical of Nadia's first ten score, was asked for her views on the two other maximum marks. 'Even great gymnasts have small imperfections,' she said. 'I am sure Comaneci and her coaches know what her weaknesses are.'

None of the reporters asked Olga about Nadia. They all wanted to know, but none dare ask. Instead, they asked if she was injured.

'No,' said Olga. 'I feel very good. But every gymnast has something that hurts. If you don't, that's when you should start to worry!'

Away from the conference, controversy was breaking out about whether any gymnast could theoretically be perfect. Boris Bajin, the Yugoslav-born national coach to Canada's women gymnasts, said that the sometimes unjustified high marks of the Russian girls on the bars had pushed Nadia's score up to ten. He said that she was unquestionably the best in the event, 'keeping higher, showing originality', but she was half a mark better than Olga Korbut. As Olga was given 9·9, that meant that Nadia ought to have received 10·4 out of 10, an impossibility.

'Theoretically, I don't think a perfect score is possible, because one can always do better. But I don't disagree with Nadia being given ten, because if anyone received 9·9, as Olga did, then Nadia had to get more. But Olga should have been marked down for holding her handstand on the high bar. To the audience, it was a sign of control. But movement on the bars has to be continuous, and if Olga had perfect control she would have swung up to 89 degrees, not 90.'

So the arguments continued. Was the marking unreasonably high, or should one expect the Olympic champion to be worth ten, and everyone else scaled down accordingly? Whatever happened to the scoring system after the Games, there were still combined exercise and individual apparatus titles to be decided later in the week, and that would give everyone a chance to assess more closely the relative merits of the various gymnasts, Nadia and Olga included.

Never before had gymnastics been such a talking point in an Olympic city, and the calmest person of all appeared to be the girl at the centre of it all, Nadia Comaneci. She now had an Olympic silver medal from the team competition, and she also had the only three perfect ten scores in Olympic gymnastics history. What she had not yet got was an Olympic gold medal.

*Chapter Nine*

## A GOLDEN DREAM COME TRUE

The next day, Tuesday 20 July, was a rest day for the girl gymnasts, although the men's voluntary exercises were taking place in the Forum. But everyone was still talking animatedly about the prospects for the next two days: Wednesday, when the women's all-round final would be held, and the Thursday when the individual apparatus finals would be decided.

On Wednesday the Montreal newspapers were reflecting the interest in Nadia and Olga too, even though the rest of the world's best gymnasts were also competing. PINT-SIZED HEAVIES TANGLE TONIGHT was the headline in one paper, which likened Nadia to the Hollywood film star Greta Garbo, always maintaining an air of mystery about herself.

The all-round competition allowed the thirty-six leading gymnasts, with a maximum of three per country from the team contest, to perform their voluntary exercises on all four pieces of apparatus again, with the new mark being added to an average of their compulsory and voluntary exercises from the team event.

The new rule, limiting each country to three gymnasts, was a controversial one, for it meant that some good gymnasts who were outside the first three in their country but still better performers than some other countries' number one girl, were left out: Elvira Saadi, for instance. But it did mean that more countries had an interest in the final – fourteen, in fact.

The gymnasts performed in groups, so that all pieces of apparatus were in use simultaneously, and it meant that the spectators had to keep a close watch on who was performing where, and a careful note of the running totals, if they were to be able to follow the overall pattern.

The atmosphere before such a competition is always emotionally charged, but given the circumstances, the personalities and the occasion, the Forum was almost alight with tension and anticipation. The theatrical build-up, with the officials marching into the arena in time with music from the speakers, and the gymnasts following from one corner of the arena, marching in step, added to this.

Some competitors would flick the odd smile of recognition towards a friend the other side of the barriers, while others would just stare straight ahead, wondering what was to befall them before they would march out again an hour or two later.

Before each group tackled a certain piece of apparatus, they were allowed their traditional warm-up period, but an element of gamesmanship creeps in at this level, and if one or two gymnasts sneak ten or fifteen seconds more than their share, the fourth and fifth gymnasts in line may find the bell ringing for the end of the warm-up before they have even started. Perhaps recognizing this, the judges sometimes allowed their attention to wander during the warm-up, so that all the gymnasts managed a few muscle-stretching exercises first and no one was left with an unfair disadvantage.

Olga began on the beam, but her mark of 9·5 seemed

a little bit on the low side, and sent the Soviet coach Larissa Latynina into a heated discussion, first with the judges and then the officials of the F.I.G. It turned out that Olga had changed part of her routine because of the ankle injury and had been marked down for inadvertently exceeding the maximum time limit of 1 min 35 secs, laid down by the F.I.G. Code of Points. A deduction of 0·3 of a mark is made for exceeding the limit and similarly a deduction is made if the exercise is shorter than the minimum of 1 min 15 secs.

Meanwhile Nadia was performing her asymmetric bars exercise perfectly once more. The lights showed another ten mark for her, the fourth of the Games, and she had now scored an incredible thirty out of thirty during her three bars appearances in Montreal. Teodora Ungureanu, who was in the same group as Nadia and Ludmila Tourischeva, scored 9·9 for her bars exercise, and so too did Nelli Kim, Marta Egervari of Hungary . . . and Olga Korbut, who was fighting back from such a disappointing start.

The high standards on the asymmetric bars, and the degrees of courage, were really eye-opening. A gymnast would only have to miss a grasp of the higher bar while performing a back somersault and she would fall uncontrollably eight or ten feet to the ground. It was horrifying to even think of the possibility, but the gymnasts were as sure in their grip as their courage.

Nelli Kim had already showed that she was likely to be a considerable threat to Nadia, if the little Rumanian came unstuck on any exercise. Already she had produced an excellent floor exercise, which included a double back somersault and some outstanding dance and tumbling elements, for a 9·95 score. That, together with her 9·9 on the bars, put her right up close to Nadia, and by scoring 9·7 for the beam she was well in the running for a medal.

So too was Ludmila Tourischeva, who – many people had forgotten – was actually defending the all-round title from the 1972 Munich Olympics. As her group moved to the vault, she pulled back a small margin on Nadia by scoring an excellent 9·95 for her high tucked Tsukahara vault. Nadia also employed a Tsukahara, but hers was piked. It scored 9·85, which was to be her lowest mark of the competition, and the group moved across to the beam.

Here Nadia pulled away again. Tourischeva was in good form, but Nadia was once more perfection. With a routine which included an aerial walkover, two consecutive flip-flops, and a double twisting somersault to dismount the 10·0 score shone yet again: the fifth time in the Games. With 29·85 out of 30·0, and just the floor exercise remaining, she could surely not be caught now.

But then a new wave of excitement shook the Forum. Nelli Kim, who had been in such great form already that evening, performed a Tsukahara vault with a full twist and landed perfectly. A pause, and then the judges decided: 10·0! So Nelli had joined Nadia in Olympic history as the only gymnast to receive a maximum score in the Games. Except, of course, that Nadia had done it five times, and Nelli once.

On the orange matting, Olga was preparing to perform her floor exercise. As she was the last competitor in round three, and knew that the audience's attention was fully on her, and that the move to the next piece of apparatus could not take place until she had finished, she was in her element: the supreme showman. It was the sort of occasion to which she rises, and she gave the exercise all she had, appealing to the audience's innermost sympathy.

Her music was the sad and wistful French tune *Milord*, which somehow seemed to fit so well with Olga's appearance, being associated as it is with another tiny, waif-like figure, singer Edith Piaf. The audience clapped in time with the music, which can be off-putting for the gymnast, but Olga responded with a good exercise which explored all the dramatic and emotional possibilities.

When her score of 'only' 9·85 went up, some sections of the crowd were loud in their disapproval, booing and catcalling, in a scene reminiscent of Munich in 1972. But the score remained unchanged. Olga, her hair tied in bunches with red and white ribbons, waved to the spectators in a gesture to thank them for their support, but she looked heartbroken. She had given her all, and this time it seemed that it was not enough. She was drained.

With just one more piece of apparatus left, Nadia was the clear leader, while Kim and Tourischeva were neck and neck with Ungureanu for the other medals. As the first competitor on the floor in this fourth and final round, Nadia was therefore following straight after Olga, and the contrast in styles was evident. Nadia's music was *Yes Sir, That's My Baby*, and again the audience responded by trying to clap in time with the music. Performing high double somersaults which drew gasps from the crowd, Nadia was in great form, almost inevitably. Her 9·9 mark confirmed what most people knew by now – that she was the outstanding girl gymnast in the world. As the gymnasts marched out of the arena, it was plain that she had won the overall title. Olga was not in the march out, though; with her ankle injury having been aggravated, she had already left the arena for treatment.

Nelli Kim had just held off Ludmila Tourischeva by 0·5 mark to take the silver medal, thanks particularly to that ten mark for her vault, while Teodora Ungureanu overtook Olga Korbut for fourth place. Gitta Escher of East Germany (6th) was the first gymnast who came from outside the two powers, Rumania and the Soviet Union, and the strength of the Eastern European countries was such that they occupied the first eleven places.

Andrea Sieger of West Germany was the first Western European (12th), while Kim Chace of the U.S.A. (14th) was the first non-European. Britain's Avril Lennox, who had done well to even get to the final stages, was 35th.

The Olympic podium was carried on to the centre of the floor exercise area, and once again the march music struck up, as the medallists came into the arena in single file, accompanied by Olympic officials. The gymnasts stood behind the podium, and then came the announcement, in French and English, which would signify the culmination of all the years of Nadia's dedication and training.

'Premiere, et championne Olympique! First, and Olympic champion! Nadia Comaneci, Rumania.'

The Forum seemed to shake with a crescendo of

cheering and applause. Nadia jumped on to the rostrum and waved both arms to the crowd. Outside the arena, Marta and Bela Karolyi were watching. At home, in Gheorghe Gheorghiu-Dej, her mother, father and brother would be watching this moment on television. So too would her schoolfriends, and all the young gymnasts with whom she trained. All over the world, other youngsters would be envying her position. It was a moment to treasure as the gold medal, on its long chain, was put round her neck. She straightened up, and once again waved both arms high to the crowd.

Nelli Kim stepped up to receive her medal, the silver, and if she was not champion, at least she had achieved a perfect ten score in the competition, and carved her own little niche in history.

Then the deposed champion, Ludmila Tourischeva, proved she was as great a sportswoman in defeat as in victory by first going round to the front of the podium to shake hands with Nadia and kiss her on the cheek before finally stepping up to receive her bronze medal.

It was an emotional moment, as it was for Nadia when she saw the Rumanian flag rise slowly to the top of the middle of the three flagpoles, and heard the strains of the Rumanian national anthem. Suddenly the realization hit her – she was Olympic champion.

Result: 1, Nadia Comaneci (Rumania) 79·275; 2, Nelli Kim (U.S.S.R.) 78·675; 3, Ludmila Tourischeva (U.S.S.R.) 78·625; 4, Teodora Ungureanu (Rumania) 78·375; 5, Olga Korbut (U.S.S.R.) 78·025; 6, Gitta Escher (East Germany) 77·750.

## Chapter Ten

## TRIPLE CHAMPION

One British journalist, covering Olympic gymnastics for the first time, said that when he arrived at the nearest underground station he had intended asking for directions to the Forum. But he didn't need to, because he was carried along on a huge tidal wave of people, all making their way there on Thursday 22 July. The final session of women's gymnastics at these Olympic Games would discover the individual champion on each of the four pieces of apparatus, and such was the interest generated by the earlier happenings that it seemed everyone in Montreal wanted to crowd into the Forum that night to see 'Little Miss Perfect'.

A twenty-minute breakdown on the underground service meant that the trains were even more like sardine tins, but the anticipation of a great evening's gymnastics made light of such discomfort for the milling fans. Outside the Forum all afternoon people without tickets were wandering up and down, calling out to no one in particular: 'Anyone got a ticket for tonight?' A few ticket touts who did have tickets were forlornly trying to find someone crazy enough to sell them some more, but they didn't bother trying to link up with the fans looking for tickets because they knew they could get a much higher price just before the event was due to begin that evening, as fans grew more and more desperate. They were right. Eventually, ten-dollar tickets were changing hands at fifteen times their face value, as the attraction of seeing Nadia in action for the last time at the Games overtook the value of money in the fans' wallets. And the more genuine the fan, the less the money seems to matter at a time like that, which is one of the few sad reflections on the excitement generated by Nadia Comaneci in Montreal.

Inside the Forum the yellow-coated security staff had already been on duty for many hours, ensuring that no gate-crashers had managed to sneak in without a ticket. Every journalist and broadcasting man or woman had their official pass checked at least three times on entering the building, and for Pressmen it meant arriving two or three hours before the competition began.

The problem was that only a limited amount of accommodation had been reserved for the press by the organizers, mainly on a first-come, first served basis. With so much world-wide interest created by the television pictures of the gymnastics, every sports editor in the world was sending his on-the-spot troops to the Forum, and the result was that the Press Box was packed to capacity about two hours before anything was due to happen in the vast arena.

It looked a funny sight, with 16,000 empty seats banked around a vacant podium, with many of the world's top names in sporting journalism jammed shoulder to shoulder in the press area, unwilling to move in case someone else came in and stole their place. In the front row, dozens of photographers with huge telescopic lenses attached to their cameras, were adjusting their focus to take in the bars, beam, floor and vaulting horses, where in a couple of hours' time the attention of the sporting world would be directed.

The organizing committee naturally did not want to expand the press area, partly because the press do not pay for their seats and therefore would be occupying places which could be sold (and money was of vital importance to the organizers, with their huge, unexpected overheads) and partly because, of course, most of the seats had already been sold long before the Games began.

So the stage was set for the individual apparatus finals, in which the leading six gymnasts on each piece of apparatus would compete once more to determine the best of each. And the only gymnast good enough to be among the field in all four pieces of apparatus was Nadia Comaneci. Even Ludmila Tourischeva had missed out on the bars, while Olga Korbut had qualified in only two pieces, the bars and the beam.

The first event to be decided was the vault, with the results to be determined by the higher score of two vaults being added to an average score from the preliminary rounds earlier in the week. Ludmila Tourischeva was the first to go. On both her vaults she took a couple of short steps on landing, but her better vault, a high tucked Tsukahara, scored 9·85.

Nadia also had a little trouble landing and scored 9·85 for a piked Tsukahara, taking several steps after a stiff-legged landing. Her second vault, a handspring with full twist, scored 9·75, so the first vault counted and was added to her preliminary average score of 9·775.

But Nelli Kim was again the oustanding vaulter.

Even though she could not match her ten of the previous day, she scored 9·95 for the same vault, this time taking a tiny step back on landing, and that score lifted her clear of the field, with Nadia finishing fourth.

> Result: 1, Nelli Kim (U.S.S.R.) 19·800; 2 equal, Ludmila Tourischeva (U.S.S.R.) and Carola Dombeck (East Germany) 19·650; 4, Nadia Comaneci (Rumania) 19·625; 5, Gitta Escher (East Germany) 19·550; 6, Marta Egervari (Hungary) 19·450.

The next apparatus was the asymmetric bars, and here Nadia once more went through her routine with its breathtaking agility and courage, including the straddled front somersault on the high bar to regrasp the same bar, front and free hip circles, handstands and stomach whips, to land perfectly with arched back and both arms straight up in the air, as the crowd rose to her. By this time, there was no question. It was as good as ever before, so it had to be ten. It was. With an astonishing *average* mark of 10·0 from the preliminary rounds, and another score of 10·0 in the final, her aggregate mark was 20·0 out of 20·0 – an Olympic record which may one day be equalled, but can never be bettered.

Teodora Ungureanu was only 0·2 of a mark behind in the totals, scoring 9·9 in the final, to take the silver medal, so Rumania were first and second. With Hungary's Marta Egervari winning the bronze, the Russian girls were out of the medals in this event for the first time for many years. Nelli Kim, the newest Olympic gold medallist, celebrated her earlier success in the worst possible way, by falling from the bars. Fortunately she was uninjured, but the chance of her doing well here had gone. Olga Korbut caught her foot on the lower bar during her routine, and the two Soviet girls were both eventually well behind the leading quartet.

Result: 1, Nadia Comaneci (Rumania) 20·000; 2, Teodora Ungureanu (Rumania) 19·800; 3, Marta Egervari (Hungary) 19·775; 4, Marion Kische (East Germany) 19·750; 5, Olga Korbut (U.S.S.R.) 19·300; 6, Nelli Kim (U.S.S.R.) 19·225.

The third competition was on the beam, and once again it was Nadia's turn to shine. With a routine which included aerial somersaults, flip-flops and a splits-leap, as well as the usual skips, dance steps and poses, ending with a double twisting somersault dismount, her seventh maximum ten score of the Olympics went up on the scoreboard. As she had led the competition before it began, with her 9·95 average from the pre-liminaries, the gold medal was decided.

Olga Korbut, with her own varied programme which did not include her famous back somersault because of her ankle injury, but ended with a full twisting dismount, came as close to perfection as at any stage during the Games. She was the defending champion in this event, but had to settle for the silver medal this time. Teodora Ungureanu added another medal, the bronze, to the Rumanian tally, by outscoring Ludmila Tourischeva – the silver medallist in 1972 – who thus finished out of the first three this year.

Results: 1, Nadia Comaneci (Rumania) 19·950; 2, Olga Korbut (U.S.S.R.) 19·725; 3, Teodora Ungureanu (Rumania) 19·700; 4, Ludmila Tourischeva (U.S.S.R.) 19·475; 5, Angelika Hellmann (East Germany) 19·450; 6, Gitta Escher (East Germany) 19·275.

And so to the final part, the floor exercise, where even an outstanding score of 9·95 for Nadia could not take her past Tourischeva or Kim, who had superior scores from the preliminaries.

Nelli Kim in fact scored another ten mark for her exercise to clinch the gold medal, while the expressive Tourischeva retained second place for the silver. Nadia once again had the audience in the palm of her hand, with her high kicks, double twisting somersaults, and her ability to interpret even musical pauses, but even another ten score would not have given her more than the bronze medal.

Results: 1, Nelli Kim (U.S.S.R.) 19·850; 2, Ludmila Tourischeva (U.S.S.R.) 19·825; 3, Nadia Comaneci (Rumania) 19·750; 4, Anna Pohludkova (Czechoslovakia) 19·575; 5, Marion Kische (East Germany) 19·475; 6, Gitta Escher (East Germany) 19·450.

Then it was all over. The accompanying pianists from the four nations concerned in the floor exercise final shook hands with each other, their work done. The gymnasts marched out, to return for the medal presentations, as twice more Nadia saw the Rumanian flag go to the top of the pole, and twice heard her national anthem. Twice more she felt a gold medal being placed around her neck, and once a bronze.

The 1976 Olympic Women's gymnastics programme was thus complete. Some tremendous performances had been seen in the arena, and new names like Kim and Ungureanu had become familiar to hundreds of millions of television viewers around the world, as they renewed their acquaintances with Ludmila Tourischeva and Olga Korbut. But the name most readily on people's lips was that of Nadia Comaneci, a girl who at fourteen years of age had, within a week, established the following Olympic honours:

Won three gold, one silver and one bronze medal;

Achieved a maximum 10·0 score never before awarded in the Olympic Games not once, but seven times;

Become Olympic all-round champion;

Become the only girl to qualify for all four individual apparatus finals, winning two of them.

Once more there was a press conference to be faced after the medals had been presented, and the journalists' interview room underneath the main stand at the Forum became more crowded and hotter than ever before as everyone waited for the appearance of Nadia. At first a harassed-looking Press Officer announced that she would not be attending the interview session that night 'because she is very tired', and a huge groan, the same in any language, went up among the world's reporters.

But later, as several Soviet gymnasts were being questioned, there was a movement at the back of the room, and in came Nadia, looking smaller, more apprehensive and bewildered than ever. Close behind her came the tall, dominating figure of coach Bela Karolyi, and they stood at the side of the room, surrounded by armed security guards who kept whispering into small walkie-talkie radios, while the Soviet press conference concluded.

Ludmila Tourischeva announced that she was retiring from competitive gymnastics, and would concentrate on coaching youngsters. But when Olga was asked whether she would be continuing until the 1980 Moscow Olympics, she turned the question around.

'Would you like me to?' she asked.

A chorus of journalists said 'Yes!'

'Then I will,' she smiled.

Then it was the turn of Nadia and coach Karolyi, who were asked once more the story of how it all began, how often Nadia trained, and so on. For many of the journalists, it was a first and only visit to gymnastics, so the questions had to be repeated. Nadia looked rather bored with it all.

'What will you do when you get back home?' asked one reporter.

'Go for a holiday at a Black Sea resort,' she answered.

She had, everyone agreed, earned it.

*Chapter Eleven*

# AFTERMATH OF MONTREAL

The Olympic Games officially ended with a huge, colourful Closing Ceremony in the Main Stadium on the evening of 1 August, and while the 80,000 crowd waited for it to begin, television pictures of some of the outstanding performers of the Games were flashed up on the giant electric scoreboards at each end of the stadium. As each of the personalities was recognized, a cheer went up, but as the figure of Nadia was shown bounding her way across the floor exercise mats, one of the biggest ovations was heard.

But Nadia was not there to hear the cheering, or even to see or take part in the Closing Ceremony. She was already back in Rumania.

The days following the gymnastics programme had been hectic indeed. She and her friend, Teodora Ungureanu, had been whisked around from place to place, meeting V.I.P.s and being interviewed in various television studios. Nadia and Teodora found it all rather overwhelming, and were happier just chatting and giggling together, like any normal teenage girls, rather than answering the same questions over and over again. Everywhere that Nadia was taken she was clutching a stuffed toy rabbit, a gift which, someone observed, appeared more valuable to her than all the medals.

Everyone wanted to see Nadia, and the star of the men's gymnastics, Nikolai Andrianov of the Soviet Union, was rather overshadowed, despite winning four gold, two silver and one bronze medal – more than Nadia.

'I'm not jealous at all,' he laughed bravely. 'People are always more interested in women than men.'

Not strictly true, of course, in most sporting circles, but it certainly seemed that the women had captured the imagination of the world in gymnastics. There was speculation as to whether at the next Olympic Games the women's finals would be the last event of the gymnastics programme, rather than the men.

Montreal, meanwhile, continued to be security-conscious. There were various bomb scares, political demonstrations and kidnap threats, and the security watch on a number of competitors, including Nadia (who was feeling homesick anyway) was tightened. So eventually it was decided that Nadia and her team-mates should return home before the end of the Games.

The news quickly got back to Rumania, where gymnastics fever was taking the country by storm. Songs and poems, celebrating the Montreal successes of the young gymnasts, were being written and broadcast, and all over the country mothers were enquiring where they could send their children to be trained as gymnasts.

On Tuesday 27 July a plane touched down at Bucharest Airport, and thousands of happy Rumanians, many holding banners and posters, surged forward on to the runway to surround it. On board were Nadia, Teodora, and the rest of the Rumanian team, and they had to stay inside for fifteen minutes, while the door of the plane remained shut and police cleared a path through the masses.

Finally the door opened, and a huge cheer went up as Nadia, Rumania's sporting queen, stepped out, dressed in her official Rumanian Olympic team outfit. Bouquets of flowers were presented to her, and police and airport officials had to hold back the crowds while the girls were taken to a nearby lounge where they could be re-united with their families and friends before facing the Rumanian press and TV reporters.

It was an emotional moment when her mother, father and brother came forward to hug her, and Nadia shed a tear or two.

For the first time she realized the effect her Montreal performances were having in Rumania. She was told how a carnival atmosphere had swept through her home town of Gheorghe Gheorghiu-Dej, and that hundreds of tourists, from Rumania and abroad, had been going to the town asking to see her house, her school, and the gymnasium where she trained. Her pictures were in all the shop windows, and all over the country people were writing to newspapers to convey their good wishes to the gymnasts 'who put themselves in the service of the Rumanian national colours with so much seriousness and effort, tenacity and patriotism.'

At the airport Nadia's mother was telling reporters: 'Nadia started gymnastics not just for performance sake, but also to consume some of her physical energy. At home she was sometimes a bit too frolicsome. But these medals are the biggest joy, the finest present, she could give us and the country she loves so dearly.'

Nadia was asked why she had come back earlier than expected, and she admitted: 'It was because I was homesick, longing to see my family and ride my bike again!' Now she was happy to be back, if just a little upset that one of her favourite dolls had lost its head in the journey back from Montreal.

In the Olympic city itself she was still a star of the Games, which were now well into their second week. A street artist, who was just putting the finishing touches to a pastel portrait of Nadia which he had copied from a magazine, found himself surrounded by tourists offering him fifty dollars for the picture.

Her face was everywhere. Prestigious American magazines like *Time*, *Newsweek* and *Sports Illustrated* all carried her picture in colour on their front covers that week. But for Nadia the Olympics were already over. She was looking forward to her holiday on the Black Sea, and then it would be back to the gym to begin preparations for the defence of her European title in the Spring of 1977.

By October of 1976 there were reports from Rumania that Nadia's weight had soared since the Olympics, and that she had put on more than a stone after returning from Montreal. There were alarms that she was getting fat, but of course all that was happening was that like any girl of her age she was becoming a woman, and her body was filling out.

The same month she gave a gymnastics display at Antibes, on the French Riviera, where Princess Grace of Monaco presented her with a gold watch. It was obvious then that the skinny, flat-chested Nadia was beginning to grow up.

In November she was voted 'World Sportswoman of the Year' by the sports editors of the European Press, gaining 343 votes, nearly 40 more than East German swimmer Kornelia Ender, who was second in the poll. But there were those people who wondered whether we would ever see Nadia again as the perfectionist gymnast. After all, they argued, her developing shape would surely change her balance on the apparatus. Other gymnasts had been forced to give up the sport after puberty because they lost some of their ability.

Their answer came later the same month, when Nadia and Teodora went to Nagoya, Japan, to compete in the Chunichi Cup competition. On 12 November, the day before it began, they were given a special birthday cake, because Nadia was fifteen years old that day and Teodora would be sixteen the next day. Together they blew out the candles, and then went on to show that they had lost nothing since Montreal.

Nelli Kim was among the competitors, but injured her shoulder and could only finish last of the fifteen participants, while Teodora took second place, scoring 39·05. But right out in front again was Nadia. She scored 9·8 on the beam, 9·95 on the vault, and a maximum of ten for the asymmetric bars and the floor exercise, for a winning total of 39·75.

In December she made a quick trip to London, not for a competition this time, but to receive the BBC Overseas Sports Personality of 1976 Award. Nadia appeared in the live *Sports Review of the Year* programme from the BBC Television Theatre at Shepherd's Bush, and a huge audience of sporting celebrities gave her a tremendously warm welcome. During the

95

programme she sat next to Olympic ice skating gold medallist John Curry, the BBC's home award winner, and himself someone who, like Nadia, had taken his sport a stage further in his Olympic victory.

After receiving her trophy from the hands of lone sailor Clare Francis, Nadia had a special message for her British fans 'I am very thankful to the BBC and my English friends. I wish you all a Happy New Year,' she said.

Everyone was delighted to see her in England, even if it was only a two-day visit. In fact, it was the first time she had ever travelled abroad simply to collect an award, instead of taking part in a tournament or display.

On her only previous visit to the U.K. she had been a totally unknown thirteen-year-old at Wembley, unexpectedly winning the 'Champions All' tournament in April 1975. Now less than two years later she was back, one of the most famous sports personalities in the world.

As she watched the video-tapes of her Montreal performances again, she must have relived it all in her mind. For in between her two visits to London she had almost stopped being Miss Nadia Comaneci. Instead, she was Little Miss Perfect.